'Jon Berry has once again written a book that sho⟨
    just the teachers weighed down by the number ⟨
the "managers" beguiled by the world of metrics.
    Orwellian world, Berry provides a gleam of h⟨
        educational principles and teacher professionalism.

**Richard Pring, Professor Emeritus, Department of Education,
University of Oxford**

'Those who think the school education policy landscape is not a
battleground are kidding themselves. Across the globe, we teachers are
working hard to retain autonomy over what happens in our classrooms
and to guard ourselves against the mostly unwarranted attentions of
politicians, bean counters and profiteers. Thank goodness Jon Berry is
on our side. His latest book will further inspire and embolden teaching
professionals everywhere to keep fighting for what they know to be true
about the ways schoolchildren are best served.'

Glenn Fowler, Secretary, Australian Education Union, ACT Branch

'Jon Berry's book is full of hope. It shows how schools can lessen the soul-
destroying effects of testmania by a simple change of mindset, putting the
quality of education rather than student outcomes at the heart of what
they do. In today's fear-filled schools this takes courage - but the more
schools do it, the more it will encourage others to do the same.'

Madeleine Holt, More than a Score

Putting the Test in its Place

Putting the Test in its Place

Teaching well and keeping the number crunchers quiet

Jon Berry

 is an imprint of

First published in 2017 by the UCL Institute of Education Press, 20 Bedford Way, London WC1H 0AL

www.ucl-ioe-press.com

©2017 Jon Berry

British Library Cataloguing in Publication Data: a catalogue record for this publication is available from the British Library

ISBNs
978-1-85856-834-8 (paperback)
978-1-85856-835-5 (PDF eBook)
978-1-85856-836-2 (ePub eBook)
978-1-85856-837-9 (Kindle eBook)

Every effort has been made to trace copyright holders and to obtain their permission for the use of copyright material. The publisher apologizes for any errors or omissions and would be grateful if notified of any corrections that should be incorporated in future reprints or editions of this book.

The opinions expressed in this publication are those of the author and do not necessarily reflect the views of the UCL Institute of Education.

Typeset by Quadrant Infotech (India) Pvt Ltd
Printed by CPI Group (UK) Ltd, Croydon, CR0 4YY
Cover image © enviromantic/iStockphoto

Contents

Acknowledgements

My thanks go to all of you who have so willingly given time to contribute to this book. I am especially grateful to the heads, teachers, staff and children who allowed me to wander so freely through your schools, watching you go about your brilliant business and letting me stick a recorder under your nose to capture your thoughts. Thanks, too, to the scores of people who seek me out to tell me stories of school and who recommend places and people to see: I am only sorry that it has not been possible to pursue all of these leads. Above all, I offer my thanks that, as with *Teachers Undefeated*, you have confirmed that the ideas behind this book are close to your hearts. I hope that I've captured your thoughts, ideas and, of course, your commitment to improve education in the way you would have wanted. To all teachers, activists and campaigners I just say this: keep at it – we have a world to win.

About the author

Dr Jon Berry is the programme director for the Professional Doctorate in Education (EdD) at the University of Hertfordshire. He taught English in comprehensive schools for 28 years before moving to the higher education sector in 2004 as a teacher educator. Since then he has pursued his research interest into teachers' professional autonomy, placing the role of the teacher against the background of the ideological drive towards marketization. His research demonstrates that despite policy overload that leaves many teachers angry, tired and bewildered at the actions of successive governments, many individual teachers and some schools still cling to a strong notion of education that genuinely puts the child at the centre. He has been an active campaigner in two education unions, the NUT and the UCU, and has been a senior lay officer in both organizations.

Foreword

The National Union of Teachers recommends this book to all of its members. They will find it an invaluable source of inspiration and information as they continue to work hard every day to make our children's education meaningful and interesting. It will also be of great interest to parents, those training to teach and anyone involved with our schools in whatever capacity.

Jon Berry's work has identified schools who have said 'it doesn't have to be this way'. It is not necessary to make testing and measurable outcomes the centrepiece of everything that happens day by day. We can provide our children with a rich, varied and creative approach to learning, confident in the knowledge that by doing so good results will follow. There is no need for them to endure a diet of coaching and rehearsal for them to learn well. The actions of the schools and teachers in this book provide living proof of this.

Our children are more than a score. This book demonstrates that two decades of high-stakes testing, constant scrutiny, and micro-management in schools has produced a situation in which young children could be seen as nothing more than data. No school, parent or child wants this to happen, but if left unchecked this insistence on measuring everything that is measurable can make it inevitable. It is also unacceptable that publishers and other commercial organizations should be using standardized testing to make profits from education because of this.

Jon argues that by using research, evidence and expert opinion – as well as citing the examples in this book – we can push back against uninformed opinion that says the only way to improve standards is to test children so often, particularly in the early years. By campaigning on all fronts in a collective and concerted way, we can provide wonderful education for our young people while putting the test firmly in its proper place.

Kevin Courtney
General Secretary, National Union of Teachers

Chapter 1

What this book is about and what it sets out to do

Tests have their place in schools and in the education of children. At the right time and in the right way it is entirely proper to have ways of finding out what children know, understand and can do. It is perfectly sensible to have benchmarks and indications so that a range of people outside the education system can understand what the attainment of particular qualifications means. What this book argues, however, is that standardized, age-related tests have now assumed such importance that it is assessment rather than learning that dictates what happens in our schools. This book argues that this does not benefit children, their parents or wider society. Tests need to be put in their proper place.

This may seem rather disconnected, but I recommend Alan Bennett's play *The History Boys* to readers unfamiliar with it. On the face of it, the educational experience portrayed is about as far removed as it is possible to be from my own – or that of tens of thousands of teachers, as they go about the enjoyable, if demanding, task of trying to get young people to learn something. The central figure is Hector, an eccentric, peculiar and marginally disreputable teacher of a certain age charged with coaching an elite group of sixth-form boys in a northern grammar school as they prepare for entrance to Oxford or Cambridge. Hector's approach to study is unconventional: he recognizes that acting out scenes from popular films is 'sheer, calculated silliness' and that his are the ramblings of 'one far gone in age and decrepitude'. Unsurprisingly, he is viewed with grudging suspicion by senior figures in the school (the play is set in an era before such figures were dubbed 'managers'). Nonetheless, the boys achieve their aim in terms of examination success and although the play's coda casts a questioning eye over the enduring value of this triumph, Hector has done what was asked of him and done it well. 'Pass it on,' he urges his charges as they leave school, referring to a love of learning and an eclecticism that should characterize education.

Even though the play shows a time, place and set of aspirations that may be unfamiliar to many teachers, its central message is one that resonates with them in their thousands. What teachers want to be able to do is meet the needs of their students and do so in a way that is lively, inventive and, on occasion, fun. This is not some *laissez-faire* abdication of responsibility on their part. Far from it: teachers understand the need to demonstrate that young people are learning and making progress and that, from time to time, they need to be assessed so that all concerned can know how they are getting along. What they do not need is to be reminded on a daily basis – sometimes even more frequently – that it is their duty to do this. What the fictional Hector knows, and what most real teachers suspect, is that if teachers are left to their own devices, children will learn and do as well as they can without a constant diet of coaching, rehearsal, and the recording of microscopic, and usually specious, indications of progress.

Readers are entitled to know why I am so confident in speaking for teachers in this way. The explanation rests with hundreds of hours of interviews with teachers, tens of thousands of words of written testimony from them – many of them unprompted – and scores of visits to schools and other settings since May 2010. At that point I had embarked on a doctoral study into teachers' professional autonomy in England. Even though the situation in England does differ from that elsewhere in the UK, the effects of globalization on education will be recognized by most teachers wherever they are from. One of the principal findings of this study was that despite the plethora of demands made on teachers in terms of data-generation, high-stakes scrutiny and the requirement to generate test results to the exclusion of practically all else, they clung to a notion of having something better to offer than the meagre, constrained diet that they felt compelled to 'deliver'. From there I wrote *Teachers Undefeated* (Berry, 2016) to take these findings to a wider audience. During the process of writing I refreshed the data from the original study by embarking on further rounds of evidence gathering. One of the most noticeable and gratifying parts of this exercise was the way in which busy teachers volunteered swathes of their time to communicate with me. This was a clear indication of the fact that teachers love talking about their practice and engaging with colleagues about it. Conversely, one of the most disappointing features of their testimony was about how the space to do so had been both literally and metaphorically closed down as staff-rooms became work-stations and meetings were subsumed with talk of data and progress. Nonetheless, the same picture emerged as from the original data: teachers harbour a notion of there being something much better on offer – for themselves as well as their students – than the narrow, restrictive approach that has emerged from educational discourse in England in the last 25 years.

With backing and support from the National Union of Teachers, *Teachers Undefeated* did reach a wide audience and I was happy to find myself speaking about it at a number of meetings and launches around the country. When we reached the point where audiences were asked to make observations or ask questions, the same ideas emerged time after time. Many teachers expressed delight at the fact that the book demonstrated to them that it wasn't just they who thought as they did; most liked the political and economic contextualization, almost all enjoyed the range of anecdotes and many furnished me with new ones. Nevertheless, they felt that something was missing – and I agree with them. Where, they wanted to know, were the schools that were prepared to be brave? Were there leaders around in the current climate who were prepared to trust teachers to do the right thing? I had cited less than a handful in the book but I had had to work hard to locate these. It was obvious that the next step was to identify more such settings and bring them, their ideas and their way of operating to this wider audience. So this current volume attempts to do just that; tell the story of individuals and settings who go about the job in a principled and pedagogically sound way, confident in the knowledge that if they continue to so, the results will follow. Some 30 years ago the notion of 'having it all' emerged from the debates around feminism; this book purloins that idea and argues that it is possible, like Hector, to have it all (maybe without the disreputable bit) by promoting learning that is lively, fun and even slightly odd, but which gets the job done.

This book is overtly political. I do not revisit the more detailed analyses of the Global Education Reform Movement (GERM), neoliberalism and the wider political and economic history that were covered in *Teachers Undefeated* – albeit that I offer brief working definitions below – but a political analysis underpins the purpose and ambition of this volume. The central thesis of this work is as follows: teachers, children and parents now find themselves involved in a system of schooling where a discourse of outcomes, results, regulation and measurement drives almost everything that goes on. None of this has happened by accident, but as result of successive – and relentless – interventions by the state as it works to control what is taught (sometimes even how it is taught) and by a need to demonstrate 'value for money' in straitened economic circumstances. For some 30 years, government involvement has been driven by an ideological commitment to the shrinking of the role of the state in the provision of public service and this currently manifests itself in promoting the privatization of such service. In schools, this is most obvious in the overt encouragement to become academies operating beyond local political and organizational control while private enterprise takes over the reins. Schools, therefore, find themselves in a situation that is reflective of dominant political imperatives that affect the way in which social provision is made and in which society overall is organized. My contention is that teachers and others need to reflect on this for two reasons. First, they need to understand how they have ended up where they are. Second, and for me as an educator and activist for 40 years this is the crucial part, they need to know how to build resistance to what is happening and in doing so make alliances with individuals, organizations and social movements whose interests they share. I completely recognize that this may not be an analysis shared by everyone – even, perhaps, many of my own interviewees or respondents. Nonetheless, one of the central messages of this book is that with confidence and certainty about their professional judgements, teachers acting collectively can bring about change – but that to do so, they need to know who and what they are up against and where to find their allies.

The definition of two ubiquitous terms that are dealt with in full in *Teachers Undefeated* will be helpful to the reader. The first of these is GERM – the Global Educational Reform Movement. The term was conceived by Finnish writer and commentator Pasi Sahlberg (see pasisahlberg.com *inter alia*) and was carefully chosen for its connotations of ill health and infection. In brief, Sahlberg's definition identifies the main features of this phenomenon as standardization of education; a focus on core subjects; low-risk ways of achieving learning goals; the adoption of corporate management models and test-based accountability policies (Sahlberg, 2012). It is a handy catch-all definition of the ills that beset education in England, and like many writers I am grateful to Sahlberg for providing it. The second of these terms is neoliberalism. For convenience, I borrow economist David Harvey's definition of the roots of neo-liberalism lying in 'the assumption that individual freedoms are guaranteed by freedom of the market and of trade' and that this assumption is 'a cardinal feature of such thinking' (Harvey, 2005: 7). Once again, the use of this terminology is something of a flag of convenience: what follows is not expert economic analysis, but an examination of teaching and learning against a broad-brush landscape of political and economic circumstance.

This leads neatly on to who this book is for. The principal audience is teachers themselves and those learning how to become teachers. I hope that teacher educators will also find it of use, particularly in conjunction with my earlier volume, and that it will prompt discussion and examination of their practice. In particular, I hope headteachers and school governors will read it. By doing so they should gain confidence from the fact that the regimes of scrutiny, observation and inspection that so inhibit and worry teachers are unnecessary; if they trust teachers to do the right thing then, with some guidance and support, results will be achieved and learners will have been able to enjoy the scenic route to the achievement of their goals. Parents, too, should find this an encouraging proposition.

This is not an academic book in the strictest sense. What readers will find, however, are numerous leads and references to various readings through which they can pursue particular interests. The breadth and diversity of the sources referenced here demonstrate a rich tradition of writing about education that challenges hegemonic positions and posits alternatives. For teachers, particularly those at the beginning of their careers, this is important at a time when a more pragmatic approach to training and professional development has resulted in the sidelining of any sustained discussion of pedagogy and policy. For the main part, the voices that readers will hear are those of current practitioners but, from time to time, I have exercised authorial privilege and have intervened with what I hope are pertinent and illustrative anecdotes from my own experience as a teacher and teacher educator – stretching now over five decades. None of these is offered in the spirit of there having been some golden age of either teaching, teacher autonomy or teacher activism. That was not the case and to argue such would be to defeat the purpose of a book whose central purpose is to look to the future.

We start with a look at the growth of the political ideology that has brought us to where we are before moving on to hear from teachers and educators themselves. The book finishes with a discussion about the necessity to campaign and argue for an education that puts children and authentic learning at the centre. Just as importantly, in a political climate that has never been more volatile and uncertain, there is consideration of what we might actively do about this. To borrow and bowdlerize from *The History Boys*, it's not good enough for us as educators to put our head in our hands and bemoan what has happened to us as one flaming thing after another; we must use our knowledge and expertise to change things for the better. I hope that this book inspires you to do so.

Chapter 2

The autonomy paradox
We'll set you free ... as long as you do what you're told

In 1988 the Conservative government passed the Education Reform Act (ERA). This influential legislation introduced the National Curriculum and, just as importantly, began the process of enabling schools in England to become independent financial entities. Many would argue, myself included (Berry, 2016), that this was the point at which the neoliberal genie was well and truly let out of the bottle. It was also the point at which the ideological drive to shrink the state in terms of social provision – a central tenet of the government of Margaret Thatcher and that of her international ally, Ronald Reagan – became obvious. Thatcher had set this particular ball rolling with one of her earliest actions as Prime Minister, which was to sell off council housing, thereby appropriating what had been public property into the private domain. Under ERA the role of local education authorities (LEAs) in England was to be diminished and the influence of these bodies reduced to that of commissioners of services rather than that of planners and providers. The path was being cleared for the open privatization of the education system embodied in The Academies Act of 2010 and the ensuing free-for-all as the open market in school provision became an article of faith for those charged with controlling our children's education.

Since 1988 the government department charged with overseeing education has been renamed on five occasions with the current label – Department for Education – a return to its assignation between 1992 and 1995. It might be tempting to see this penchant for renaming and re-branding as a metaphor for what has happened in schools during this period, as teachers and pupils are subjected to whichever trend or magic bullet holds favour at the time. In the 28 years since ERA there have, at the time of writing, been 14 secretaries of state: eight Conservative and six Labour. Only one of these post-holders was ever a teacher. Estelle Morris (Labour) held office for 16 months – not quite the shortest tenure during this period – before resigning (the only secretary of state for education to do so) in October, 2002. The lack of understanding and empathy from senior politicians emerges as a frequent complaint from teachers frustrated by what they see as the constant need for politicians to remind them of their professional obligations and, as a consequence, to intervene in a harmful and obstructive way (Berry, 2016). The fact that so few of them know and understand the daily workings of schools reinforces this resentment and is a theme that recurs in many of my conversations with them.

Although some of the 14 post-holders went on to the greater offices of state (education is not deemed to be of sufficient importance to be so designated) many sank without trace. That could not be said of Michael Gove – notwithstanding his temporary dart for political glory in June 2016. Appointed in May 2010 he was removed from office in July 2014, by which time he was deemed by government advisers to be a 'toxic liability' among teachers (Watt and Wintour, 2014). His period in office was the longest since ERA and, indeed, the longest for well over 60 years. During that time his influence on schools and teachers was profound. As I now go on to argue, it was also ideologically driven to an extent that needs to be carefully examined if we are to understand where schools currently find themselves and, just as importantly for this book, how resistance to the ideas that drove him need to be nurtured and changes put in place.

Gove took office in May 2010. A few weeks earlier, at the conference of the Association of Teachers and Lecturers (ATL), he had told teachers that 'the Conservative Party will give you freedom to teach how you want to' (ATL, 2010). Once elected, he wrote in the foreword to the government's white paper on education of his immense admiration for teachers: 'there is no calling more noble, no profession more vital, and no service more important than teaching' (DfE, 2010). How is it possible that someone capable of expressing such positive sentiments could be deemed a 'toxic liability' some four years later?

The answer lies in the political imperative that informed the thinking of Gove and his supporters. For an indication of just how strong that imperative was it is worth looking at the extraordinary speed with which the new government framed and introduced legislation pertaining to schools. Within three months of taking office, the Academies Act was on the statute books. To put this in perspective, this rush to completion meant that the Terrorism Prevention and Investigation Measures Bill was left unratified for another five months while measures allowing – in truth, encouraging – schools to become academies was scooted through the system with unprecedented haste (Berry, 2012). The justification for this haste was cleverly couched in language that, on the surface, might well seem appealing to teachers, headteachers and anyone interested in schools. Academy schools would be the very epitome of freedom and independence from central control. Reinforcing the admiration for teachers and the job they do expressed earlier in the foreword, an even more encouraging passage follows:

> Ministers are committed to giving schools more freedom from unnecessary prescription and bureaucracy. They have always made clear their intentions to make changes to the National Curriculum that will ensure a relentless focus on the basics and give teachers more flexibility that the proposed new primary curriculum offered.
>
> (DfE, 2010)

On the face of it, what could be better? A 'noble', valued profession, set free to teach how it likes in settings free from prescription and bureaucracy.

In order to explain the ironies and paradoxes that undermine this apparently benign set of intentions, we need to look closely at this far-reaching piece of legislation. The reader will need to bear with me as I pick through what may seem, initially, to be some dry statistics: they help to piece together a revealing backdrop to what has happened in classrooms on a daily basis since 2010. The Academies Act (for those bedevilled by insomnia, it is available at legislation.gov.uk) consists of 20 provisions over the same number of pages. Curricular provision is mentioned once, teachers are not mentioned at all and the three references to headteachers are all in terms of them becoming 'proprietors' of schools. The Act concerns itself almost exclusively with the apparatus of establishing schools as independent financial entities. The powers of the Secretary of State are mentioned on 51 occasions and there are ten provisions for the transfer of land, as well as other fiscal and organizational responsibilities, away from local authorities; six of these deal exclusively with the ceding of these powers to the new 'proprietors'. Such consultation as is required for conversion to academy status need only take place with such persons deemed appropriate by the governors of the school that is seeking to do so. In other words, this is about facilitating the privatization of education and absolutely nothing to do with teaching and learning. Some six years later when the chancellor of the exchequer, George Osborne, announced that the government now insisted that all schools become academies, he did so in his budget speech. Like Gove, he used the language of 'freedom':

> First, I can announce that we are going to complete the task of setting schools free from local education bureaucracy, and we're going to do it in this Parliament.
>
> (Osborne, 2016)

Many teachers were puzzled by this on two counts. First, why was what was once voluntary now becoming compulsory? As it happens, concerted opposition to this flawed move caused a retraction from the government within weeks. Second, why was a measure concerned with education policy being introduced in the Budget? Osborne's speech makes it clear: a 'fair funding formula' will be put in place enabling schools to operate free from this burdensome bureaucracy. The message is clear; let's hand over financial arrangements to those who are so much better placed to put government funds to best use.

When talking of the fundamental paradox of neoliberalism, Harvey (2005) points out that its proponents distrust the state and, in particular, its intervention in social policy. Its supporters believe that state intervention runs counter to the primacy of market forces and the ability of these forces to deliver a level of service that is effective and which provides value for money. At the same time, however, for such an ideological position to hold sway, the state itself has to create the very circumstances that privilege such an approach. In this instance, a central diktat strips control of education away from democratically elected local bodies that are accountable to local communities and places 51 powers of intervention in the hands of a remote, centrally located Secretary of State. Meanwhile, land and property that were once locally owned are brazenly handed over to the 'proprietors' and, of course in some cases, their sponsors. Writing in 2011, academic Clyde Chitty characterized this perfectly, calling it a 'massive power grab from local communities' (Chitty, 2011). Put baldly, the freedom of the market to operate public services is only in place because of the will of a government prepared to enforce the circumstances in which such 'freedom' can be given licence to operate.

When forensically examined, the actions of these new 'proprietors' as they seize the chance to run our schools is breath-taking. I am grateful in this to the work of Matthew Bennett (2016). What Gove started with the Academies Act his successors developed with the Education and Adoption Act of 2016 (UK Government, 2016). The Act sets out to remove the influence of governors and, in particular, parent and teacher governors or anyone associated with local authorities. It talks of streamlining and professionalizing governing bodies to the point where 'as we move towards a system where every school is an academy, fully skills-based governance will become the norm'. The government minister charged with school governance at the time of introducing this legislation was Lord Nash. Nash and his wife, a former stockbroker, run a small academy chain in Westminster and sit on the board of the 'flagship' Pimlico Academy. His view of how schools should be run is crystal clear: 'running a school is in many ways like running a business, so we need more business people coming forward to become governors' (Bennett, 2016). Nash is also co-founder of Sovereign Capital, a private equity firm, which recently acquired the Alpha Plus Group that markets itself as 'one of the UK's most prestigious private education companies'. Sovereign Capital currently invests in Paragon, a work-based training provider that received £17 million from the government in 2016. And so the list and the connections go on and on ... of major companies like JPMorgan Chase and KPMG all hovering round to see what is to be gained from the open market that the governance of schools now presents. And all of this is a testament to deliberate and ideologically driven decision-making by those charged with running the state.

Over the years I have had conversations with many valued colleagues working in schools who have expressed frustration at what they see as double-standards or muddled thinking on the part of Gove, his successors, and his parliamentary colleagues. They express astonishment that ministers don't seem to be able to spot the irony here: on the one hand we're being told to be free, on the other, the only accountability seems to be to a centralized authority. Unfortunately, my colleagues underestimate the force of the ideological drive in play here. By making outcomes and results the principal factors determining the success or otherwise of a school what need do we have of localized controls? Tie these successful outcomes to a public profile that makes an institution more popular and marketable, why should we bother with pesky planning and equitable provision? Parents, we are asked to believe, can decide and make choices about where to send their children based on these outcomes – conveniently forgetting the one in seven who can't (Weale, 2016). The creation of a competitive, fractured and non-co-operative system that generates winners and losers is part of the very fabric of neoliberalism and its correspondence with market forces. The language may be about independence and freedom but the intent is about the state handing that which was public to those who can profit by these arrangements.

The question for schools and teachers is about how this relates to their daily work. I hope I am not being insulting to people with whom I've worked and co-operated for the last 40 years or so when I say that in the hurly-burly of a working day in school, if it's a case of evaluating the thrust and purpose of government policy in the light of economic imperatives or making sure that things are in place for the next lesson with a room full of demanding youngsters, political analysis takes a back seat. Nevertheless, it is these very economic and political drivers that play out in the classroom in a whole range of ways. I illustrate this with an anecdote from my professional practice.

As part of my professional duties, I am charged with conducting final observations of training teachers from institutions other than my own. I find myself in a school in another part of the country to see a student teacher whom I have not previously met. The school itself is located in an area of clear economic and social deprivation. The buildings are new and clean – the school has recently undergone conversion to an academy – and it appears to be well resourced. I am to watch a young man teach a Year 10 class (14 and 15-year-olds) that is studying Information and Computer Technology (ICT). The class enter in orderly fashion, exchange low-key pleasantries with the teacher, log on to their computers and generally seem ready to start work in a purposeful way. I note all of this as being extremely positive and testament to the working relationship that this young teacher has established with his class. What is more, he has taken an apparently dry subject about computer images and has worked this so that the class will be looking at body-image in advertising. Again, I note this with approval. What happens in the five minutes that follow is less encouraging. With the class set up and ready to work, he embarks on an explanation of how the work they will be doing today will help them to boost their grades from Ds to Cs. To reinforce the message, he projects the grade criteria on to the whiteboard. He soldiers on with his explanation while the class take not one blind bit of notice. They do not misbehave or chatter; many of them try to get on with their work, almost surreptitiously. And once again, I credit him with having established this positive working atmosphere.

With the explanation of criteria completed, he continues with the lesson, which is a good one. The class make sensible observations about the use of 'perfect' body images and how these are used to manipulate readers and viewers. It is fair to say that there is plenty of good-natured and risqué comment about the models used in the material they are exploring. The teacher has a firm and friendly manner and the potential for anything getting out of hand is confidently controlled. As the lesson draws to its close, he begins to recap ... by talking about how today's work will help them ensure that they get a C grade. Once again, no-one listens.

At the end of the lesson we talk about what has happened. I ask him for his reaction and his immediate response is to say that he spent too long talking. I am interested in this reaction and push him on it a little: I explain that, for the main part, I thought his interventions were well chosen and helpful. He agrees, but says – astutely – that there were parts of the lesson where the class was not listening to him. We both identify that these were the points at which he was explaining the importance of grade criteria. He then explains what I already knew: he is obliged to top and tail each of his lessons with this script in case he is subject to an impromptu visit from senior colleagues – the 'learning walk'. They will check that he has delivered this message and may well check that he has done so by asking one of the students in the class if this has happened. Curiously, I find myself, too, glancing at the door as we both bemoan the fact that this practice, deemed by the school's managers to be non-negotiable for all examination classes, must become increasingly meaningless for all students as they move from lesson to lesson throughout the day.

What prompts this absurd situation, whereby a school insists on teachers saying silly things that anyone with a week's experience in school knows that students will ignore, is the pursuit of results and outcomes. It is impossible to overestimate the extent to which chasing these 'outcomes' has dominated what happens in educational settings at all stages from the early years until the end of compulsory education. A great deal of the testimony in *Teachers Undefeated* spoke of how the pursuit of test results dominates everything that happened in schools, with many teachers clearly identifying the central paradox of being told that they were at liberty to act autonomously while working in a febrile atmosphere where the generation of results dominated institutional discourse. With this in mind, it is worth reiterating an important argument from that earlier book.

No teacher is opposed to assessment. It's what we do: we need to find out what children know, understand and can do and, having done so, move them onwards to greater things. When it comes to national tests, particularly qualifications to be gained at the age of 16 and 18, teachers are duty-bound to work with students to get the best results they can because, in many cases, these results do have an effect on the chances of young people. As a secondary teacher myself I spent plenty of time in the period immediately prior to public examinations furnishing my students with every hint, trick and technique to garner every last mark from their test questions. Not to have done so would have been an abdication of my responsibility towards them – and, what is more, neither I nor my colleagues ever needed anyone on a learning walk to remind us of this obligation. Most teachers enter the profession precisely because they want children to flourish and many do so in the hope that they will imbue young people with the same love of subject and learning that inspired them to become teachers in the first place. Finding out how well children are doing – assessing them – is central to the process.

All of this is a world away from what the term 'assessment' has now come to mean for teachers and schools in England in the second decade of the 21st century. What makes matters even worse is a pseudo-science that has been developed around assessment; in particular, the worthy, but often grotesquely applied notions of self and peer assessment. In 1998, Paul Black and Dylan Wiliam wrote the important and influential essay *Inside the Black Box* (Black and Wiliam, 1998), in which the notion of formative assessment, now properly installed as part of the repertoire of all good teachers, was clearly articulated. Similarly, the concept of Assessment for Learning (AfL) was formulated and promoted by the same writers. There is little doubt that these entirely unexceptionable notions have improved the practice and understanding of thousands of teachers. What is less encouraging is how these ideas have been taken up in formulaic and unthinking ways by school leaders and managers as they attempt to measure the learning process so that 'progress' can be demonstrated. The following illustration is illuminating.

In an echo of the earlier anecdote in this chapter, a colleague who leads a course for training primary school teachers tells me of an episode during a lesson observation. A group of Year 5 children (9 to 10-year-olds) are to write a set of instructions for making a mask: a perfectly proper and sensible piece of writing for a specific purpose. They are arranged into groups in order to work collaboratively; so far, so good. The first thing the teacher asks them to do is to identify some success criteria for the task ahead. Although perhaps a touch cumbersome, my colleague recognizes that sharpening up the focus of the writing task may be no bad thing. But once these criteria have been identified they are to take out a purple 'polishing' pen and refine these criteria. Eventually, some mask-making instructions are written. Readers at this point might be forgiven for thinking that the next stage would be to take the instructions and see whether or not a suitable mask could be made from them. But no. First, the teacher is obliged to look at the criteria, identifying 'pink' areas for possible improvement and 'green' for ideas that pass muster. Any mask-making yet? Not quite. Children now have to peer-assess their classmates' work with comments that recognize success or suggest improvement. And so, at the end of a writing lesson, we have purple, pink and green comments by way of self and teacher assessment and an evaluation as a form of peer assessment. Anything more clearly designed to make children see writing as a cumbersome and pointless exercise is difficult to imagine; but we have had more assessment than any one individual could ever wish for. The fact that it has probably not aided anyone's learning or understanding is immaterial: assessment, of all sorts, has taken place. What is more, there is 'evidence' that it has happened. Such evidence is vital if outcomes are to be properly measured.

Such episodes – and I know from the huge volume of testimony from teachers how frequent they are – are at the centre of the autonomy paradox. If the ideological thinking behind the provision of education is informed by the notion that it is a commodity on the open market and that schools have to prove their value and attractiveness in these terms, then the way in which this value can be demonstrated must be through the production of results. As a consequence, these results assume an importance that subsumes all other considerations such as, for example, the provisions made for children with particular needs or the degree of pastoral care offered, particularly in areas of social deprivation. Tie this in with a system of performance-related pay for teachers and a permanent institutional nervousness about what a poor report from the Office for Standards in Education (Ofsted) can mean, then this begins to explain why a perfectly simple lesson about framing a few instructions ends up being a fragmented display of ill-judged assessments instead of the fun of making a good mask.

One further way in which the autonomy of schools and teachers is threatened is the narrowing of what is taught and the way in which some subjects are endowed with greater importance than others. In this the extent to which the ideological predilections of those who control state education are accommodated needs to be understood. As far back as 1971 the content of the school curriculum was exercising politicians – most specifically those with rightward leanings. Characterized by many academics as the New Right (Johnson, 1991), much of their thinking is echoed by Gove and his successors. The narrative created by the New Right played well in the popular press. Schools and teachers were frequently portrayed as having abandoned Shakespeare for soap operas, Beethoven for reggae and religious education for vague and unfocused discussion of multi-culturalism and anti-sexism (Cox, 1995). One of the central figures in New Right thinking was London headteacher Rhodes Boyson who articulated what Johnson describes as an a nostalgic hankering for the 'strong dependable grammar school ... complete with mental and moral disciplines, blazers, badges (and) corporal punishment' (Johnson, 1991: 39). We have a flavour of this when Boyson writes:

> We shall not improve the quality of education in this country
> until we return to a sense of purpose, continuity and authority in
> our general attitude to life and society.
>
> (Boyson, 1975: 137)

Boyson along with others had been instrumental in the writing of the *Black Papers* between 1969 and 1971 (Cox and Dyson, 1971). The Papers expressed opposition to teacher-led examinations and the growth of comprehensive schools as well as voicing concerns about unfettered freedom in junior schools and worries that the move to comprehensive schools set the nation on the road to a Soviet Russian system that was already a proven failure (Szamuely, 121–38, in Cox and Dyson, 1971).

All of which would now seem somewhat fanciful had such thinking disappeared into the mists of time. Far from having done so, much of what informed the New Right nearly half a century ago is easily recognizable in current government policy in England. Nowhere does this manifest itself as starkly as in the centrality of two features of school-life: the so-called English Baccalaureate (DfE, 2016b) for 16-year-olds and the new Standardized Assessment Tests (SATS) at Key Stage 2 (KS2) for pupils about to enter the secondary sector at 11 years old. The first of these was, like so much of current policy, mooted within the first moments of the installation of the coalition government in May 2010. The English Baccalaureate was a confection that meant that such an award could only be bestowed on students who had been successful in examinations in 'rigorous' subjects such as English, mathematics, science, foreign languages, and traditional humanities such as history or geography. (Let us be clear here: this is NOT to deny that a grasp of literacy and numeracy are essential accomplishments.) Much of this panders to perennial right-wing concerns about what are perceived as easy and worthless examinations, with the right's irrepressible *bête noire*, media studies, cited as the prime example (see, for example, Harris, 2014). The effect of this is to establish a hierarchy of subjects in terms of their value to the institution and its published results: this determinant is not necessarily of value to the individual student. Subjects such as art and drama or other areas that encourage creativity or manual dexterity or physical ability take second-place to traditional areas of study – in which, of course, their advocates themselves were successful. The entrenchment of this hierarchy of subjects in English secondary schools is captured brilliantly in the comical story of the buckets in *Teachers Undefeated* (p.53) in which a meeting of senior leaders attaches importance to filling the buckets representing some subjects at the expense of others. To reiterate the point made by the respondent who tells me of this – I am not pulling the reader's leg.

This privileging of some subject areas over others begins in primary schools. It is worth restating the point that no teacher would ever argue about the central importance of teaching children to read, write and be numerate and to develop these skills to the highest level of which they are capable. There is, however, no pedagogical research or precedent that supports an approach to the education of very young children that relegates play, experimentation, failure (heaven forbid!) or the pursuit of the peculiar in favour of an unbalanced diet of 'literacy and numeracy'. None of which is to suggest that there aren't many schools out there who are working hard to make such a diet more palatable to children. In a charming episode at my own place of work, a student teacher (I doggedly attempt to avoid the term 'trainee') bounds up to me in the corridor. She has heard my lecture in which I have questioned the rigidity of the curriculum and she has something wonderful to tell me. In her school, she informs me, they pick a topic – in this case, China – and they do all the reading, writing, science, art and humanities around this. She is enthralled by this and I, too, express my admiration: I forebear to tell her that that's what Mrs Kay used to do in my primary school in Birmingham nearly 60 years ago and I reaffirm this is certainly the sort of model of learning that should get children engaged and keep teachers happy. But many schools operate in a way that is far removed from tailoring the curriculum to meet the needs of children. Instead, a great deal of energy is expended on ensuring that children's writing is peppered with connectives, adverbial phrases, exclamatory sentences or modal verbs – all of which can, no doubt, be measured and counted up so that we can tell how well a child writes.

This narrowing of the curriculum to what can be measured and tabulated is firmly entrenched and has been for some 20 years. It represents a triumph of political ideology and dogma over professional experience and expertise. It has had a profound effect on what is taught and what children are able to learn. It has had an effect on the wellbeing of students and teachers and their relationship with each other (Hutchings, 2015). It has created a situation where attrition rates from teaching are alarmingly high and where unnecessary workload is identified as the prime factor of dissatisfaction in a job that, otherwise, teachers say they love (Lightfoot, 2016). None of this matches up to Gove's promise of freedom to teach 'how you want to' or 'freedom from prescription and unnecessary bureaucracy'. As experienced teacher Shaun puts it so pithily in one of my early interviews with him:

> So whilst you say that teachers are free to teach what they want
> in their own direction, unfortunately the direction's already set in
> stone and therefore you have to just arrive at the destination that
> somebody else has made for you.

The American economist Harry Braverman captured the ideological provenance of this situation perfectly when he wrote of how managerial systems allow workers to 'have the illusion of making decisions by choosing among fixed and limited alternatives designed by a management that deliberately leaves insignificant matters open to choice' (Braverman, 1974: 39). The academic Michael Apple has argued for the last five decades that the curriculum is an ideological construct and that good teachers have always done their best to subvert its attempt to control their actions as they go about their daily business (see, for example, Apple, 2004 *inter alia*). He points to the fact that especially in times of financial crisis, governments will attempt to intensify the demands made on workers and that such intensification leads, inevitably, to the proliferation of management systems, the use of pre-specified competencies and a predilection for standardized testing. As Ball (2008: 47) observes, in such situations it is unsurprising that 'the manager (becomes) the cultural hero of the new public service paradigm'. Even as recently as 2008, Ball would not have recognized the clipboard-wielding proponent of the learning walk or the book trawl, but burgeoning managerialism and teacher performativity sit at the centre of a situation where any conception of genuine autonomy remains very limited.

All of which might be designed to make even the most optimistic of educators crawl under a stone and hide *if* we all believed in what was being foisted on us. Fortunately that is not the case. This chapter has attempted to place the argument about the autonomy of teachers and their schools in a firmly political and ideological context and in doing so reaffirm the basic theoretical position put forward in *Teachers Undefeated*. I do not pretend that such thinking informs that of the hundreds of teachers I have now interviewed or who have provided me with tens of thousands of words of written testimony or who have invited me to their schools to see their practice and to speak to me about it. What I remain entirely confident about, however, is that to borrow again from Ball (2003) – the soul and the spirit of teachers has not been captured. What this book now sets out to do is to find the oases and the alternatives. This is a search that follows logically from the optimism of teachers who want their hopes confirmed. Can we have it all? Can we genuinely teach how we want to and still be confident that we'll get the results that will keep these 'heroic' managers happy?

Chapter 3

Seven different schools and one happy outrider

The challenge in writing this book, as explained in the first chapter, was set for me by other people. One of the principal purposes of *Teachers Undefeated* was to demonstrate to the teachers who read it that they were not on their own; there were others who felt that they had more to offer than was tolerated by current constraints. As a follow-up to what that book revealed, many teachers contacted me to say that they wanted to know if there were whole schools who felt the same way – and that was the challenge that I took up when embarking on this project. Finding such schools and, in particular, finding schools who were able to respond to my initial requests for visits turned out to be every bit as difficult as I anticipated. There was no shortage of recommendations from colleagues and professional networks, all of which were followed up, but actually managing to confirm visits and put them in place, even from schools who expressed genuine interest in the project, was often a step too far in a world where demands of all sorts pour into schools on an hourly basis. In such circumstances, I express my great gratitude to those schools that found time and space for me.

Before I explain the procedures and practices that underpin the data collection for this book, there is an illuminating tale to tell about one school that was indeed happy to have me visit and which responded with alacrity to my email request. A free school established under recent legislation, it is listed with Companies House as a private limited company with fully transparent accounts. The school has enjoyed some national acclaim for its innovatory curriculum and has been the subject of numerous favourable media reports. Independently of each other, and notwithstanding their antipathy to the ideological drive behind free schools, a number of colleagues suggested it might prove of interest to me. I emailed the school and, given its high current profile, I was pleasantly surprised to receive an email by return expressing interest in the research and inviting me to visit with some suggested times and dates. What then came as something of a shock was the request for a fee of £250 for doing so. I wrote back explaining that there may be some misunderstanding and that I wished to visit the school for reasons of academic research but the fee remained non-negotiable. When the market comes to some schools, it appears, it is applied to everything with which it comes into contact.

Seven schools, however, were happier to act in a more collegiate way with a fellow professional. Two of these – dubbed here as Grace and Hope as they were in the original publication – offered themselves by way of a follow-up to previous research done there. The other five are a mixture of recommendations and responses to contacts made through various professional networks. Ultimately, this is a self-selected group of four primary and three secondary schools. Also included is a visit to a home school setting – and I implore readers to be patient here before dismissing this as crankiness. This element of self-selection of respondents is correspondent to the notion of purposeful sampling, identified in Patton's seminal explanation of this research approach:

> The logic and power of purposeful sampling lies in selecting information-rich cases for study in depth. Information-rich cases are those from which one can learn a great deal about issues of central importance to the purpose of the research, thus the term purposeful sampling.
>
> (Patton, 1990: 169)

Patton goes on to explain that such an approach allows the researcher to 'manifest the phenomenon of interest intensely (but not extremely)' (Patton, 1990: 171). Unlike probability sampling, which usually involves greater numbers of participants, no great claim is made about generalizability from such an approach. Given the nature of this particular project, which is to identify schools that do not conform to current norms, this is not regarded as a problem here.

The other issue relating to the conduct and reliability of any research project is that of a potential conflict when an 'insider' takes the lead. Although not a schoolteacher, I consider myself such an insider. For nearly 30 years I was a teacher, opting to work in state comprehensive schools. I was an active campaigner against the imposition of national testing in the early 1990s and have remained so since. When I became a teacher educator in 2004, I remained adamant that teachers should bring a critical and analytical eye to what they were being asked to do in school and not take the path of least resistance – 'because they'll be tested on it'. My own doctoral research was prompted by concern that a regime of testing, measurement and the commodification of education could have a deleterious effect on how teachers went about their business. This accumulated experience makes me an insider. It does not, however, preclude the possibility of researching an issue with clarity and criticality:

> In considering insider-research projects, potential researchers, through a process of reflexivity, need to be aware of the strengths and limits of their preunderstanding so that they can use their experiential and theoretical knowledge to reframe their understanding of situations to which they are close.
>
> (Brannick and Coghlan, 2007: 72)

There is no claim in the reporting that follows that the researcher is a detached ethnographer, and I do bring 'preunderstanding' of some sort to the situation. As Brannick and Coghlan identify, however, it is the careful placing of these understandings within the theoretical framework of education as a marketized and marketable commodity that brings the necessary reflexivity to the research itself. In short, I cannot shake off my teacher identity, but that does not mean that I am unable to bring an analytical perspective to what I see and hear.

The eight settings are willing, even eager, participants. The work done in three of the schools can also be characterized as co-constructional with teachers and school leaders being keen to share thoughts and analyses after the visit to inform their future actions. This openness is reflected in how the visits and various correspondence about them took place. In the case of five of the schools, the principal correspondent was the headteacher: in the other two, it was a senior leader acting on the head's behalf. In all cases, having explained the purpose of the research, I made it clear that I was at the school's disposal in terms of what I saw and where I went, but that I did not wish to see anything other than a 'normal' school day in progress. I made it clear that I would be grateful if teachers could find some time to talk to me individually or in groups but that I realized that during such a 'normal' day this might not be possible. Timetables and plans were then put in place and the visits themselves took place between October 2016 and January of the following year.

As the reader will discover in what follows, there are characteristics common to all these visits. In all cases I was told to walk around as I pleased and to talk to anyone – teachers, other staff, children, parents and visitors – when it was convenient to do so. There is a need for care about how I express the next common factor: in no cases did I see anything spectacular, special or out of the ordinary. What I mean here is that I saw teachers and children getting on with the everyday business of teaching and learning. There were no special, one-off lessons and, apart from one brief instance, no outside visitors or special events. This speaks of great confidence and certainty from the schools themselves: the message seems to be that to see us at our best just see us going about our normal business. I make the point unapologetically in many instances that follow; making the demanding business of teaching and learning look so unspectacular is a genuine accomplishment.

During the course of these visits, I spoke to six headteachers and 67 teachers in either individual or group interviews all of which were audio-recorded. I had numerous brief, casual conversations with teachers and a range of other adults, including parents at school gates, assistants at breakfast clubs and administrative staff, almost all of which were not recorded and, as such, have not been quoted verbatim in the following chapters. There is some reference back to the research that informs *Teachers Undefeated*, which draws on the testimony of more than 100 teachers (see Berry, 2016, Chapter 3). Anonymity has been preserved in all cases with the use of pseudonyms or playful names for establishments. There is one instance where the preservation of this anonymity has been difficult but the key individuals are comfortable with this situation. The final chapter includes materials gathered from interviews with named individuals, all of whom are happy to be identified.

These seven schools are not the only ones who are making a collective, institutional statement about their resistance to the current hegemony of relentless, high-stakes accountability. It would be absurd to make such a claim. Late in the course of this project I was alerted to two other schools that, in the opinions of the interviewee, would have fitted the bill in terms of their view of testing and who would probably have been happy to have invited me to see them in action, but circumstances prevented this from taking place. The chosen schools happen to be some examples that illustrate that resistance to the global education reform movement (GERM) is possible. Although some individuals who work in these schools see their opposition to the prevalence of GERM in ideological terms, most do not. Very few respondents frame their concerns in overtly political terms, other than to bemoan the perceived ignorance and detachment of government intervention that, in itself, is couched in general, rather than party-political, terms. It is equally important to make the point that the vast majority of schools – those that choose the path of conformity and compliance – are not dupes and weaklings. In more than 40 years of working with schools, heads and teachers, I have yet to come across anyone who thought they were setting out to do the wrong thing by their pupils and students. As my research from the last seven years illustrates, teachers carry with them a finer idea of what education can offer than that allowed in most settings and situations. The fact that circumstance impinges on such schools so that they become unwilling or unable to carry through such convictions does not mean that those who work there lack principles or commitment to young people.

We start by looking at a range of compelling evidence and argument that reinforces the notion of putting testing in its place. From there we look at the primary sector – I do hope that those with an interest in secondary schools don't skip this, there's a lot to like and learn – before moving on to secondary schools. In Chapter 8 we return to a very special primary school before looking at alternative provision and then at possibilities for resistance and a way forward in the final chapter.

Chapter 4

The mismeasurement of learning

The experts' view

There is no evidence to demonstrate that testing improves standards. This inconvenient truth has bedevilled a succession of politicians for more than a quarter of a century as they insist on intoning this 'common-sense' mantra to justify the 'rigour' they demand from our schools. The reaction to criticism from many politicians in recent years has been to discredit the bearers of messages that are unpalatable. For example, during the Brexit campaign in 2016, Michael Gove, by then removed from his responsibility for education, expressed the view that the people of Britain had 'had enough of experts' (YouTube, 2017). This was an echo of a view expressed in his former role that 'there is some evidence that university-based trainees see their training as too theoretical' (DfE, 2011: 14). The source of any such evidence is not cited. The insuperable problem for Gove, his successors, and predecessors has been that the overwhelming weight of informed opinion is not on their side. When faced with such uneven odds, sneering at opponents (Gove's favourite sobriquet for academics involved with education is The Blob) appears to be their only course of action. Fortunately for children, teachers, schools and parents, these critics have been undeterred. It is to the great discredit of those who are scornful of peer-reviewed academic comment that it is often derided as making excuses for failure or informed by some misguided sense of equality or, that worst of all evils, 'political correctness' – again, shorthand for 'a view that challenges my/our own'.

Some of the work of such academics is captured in *The Mismeasurement of Learning* (Berry and Wrigley, 2016). What follows in this chapter draws, with gratitude, from the efforts of colleagues, all of whom persevere with research and scholarship whose purpose is to improve the learning and development of young people. When referring to colleagues' work in the following paragraphs, I have done so simply by using their names: a simple search of the contents list of this publication will identify the individual articles from which quotations are taken.

Pam Jarvis from Leeds Trinity University bemoans the fact that 'despite a century of empirical and theoretical advances ... the state education system has never become sufficiently informed about the human developmental process' and has reduced such a process to 'a simple insistence that the earlier children enter education and the faster they are expected to learn, the better the outcome will be'. She cites the work of Professor Alison Gopnick whose copious empirical data support her view that formal instruction in early childhood 'leads children to narrow in and to consider just the specific information that a teacher provides' thereby inhibiting a child's natural inclination to look for a greater range of options. The outcome of this reductive view of how learning takes place is illustrated in the teachers' comments, collected and reviewed by Ken Jones, formerly professor of education at Goldsmiths, about the 2016 national tests for primary school children. These tests were revamped in 2016 as a result of governmental interference to make them more demanding. Even when putting aside difficulties arising from leaked examination papers and poor administration, this quest for higher standards through stiffer testing led to some alarming outcomes. Forty-seven per cent of pupils failed to reach the 'expected standards' at age 11 in reading, writing and mathematics. Twice as many Year 1 children born in August, the youngest in their school year, failed the phonics test – to which we will return – as those born in the previous September. The attainment gap between children receiving free school meals – the accepted indicator for disadvantage – doubled between 2015 and 2016. Jones reports that 97 per cent of teacher respondents to a survey about their experience of the SATs agreed that preparation for these tests had had a negative impact on children's access to a broad and balanced curriculum. Ninety per cent believed that the testing regime had a negative experience on children's overall experience of education and 97 per cent believed that arrangements for testing had been poorly managed. The terms 'shambles' or 'shambolic' are used more than 100 times in responses along with frequent reference to 'chaos', 'fiasco' and 'farce'.

As John Coe of the National Association for Primary Education explains, this unseemly mess stems from what he dubs 'three myths about assessment'. The first of these is that harder tests raise standards of achievement. When more difficult tests are imposed, learning is removed from assessment, especially in a system where the high-stakes importance of achieving outcomes is so prevalent. Coaching, rehearsal and repeated test-practice – all of which are superficial activities encouraging no depth of learning – become the order of the day. The idea of pitching what is tested *above* the heads of many children is a peculiar way to assess what they actually do understand. Second, Coe challenges the notion that test results are accurate as a measure of progress through school. Testing can only ever be a snapshot at a given moment and can only test what is inherently measurable. Even the most comprehensive set of examinations – and the national tests with their narrow range of subjects do not fit that description – cannot identify any individual's potential for development. To do so requires a holistic approach to assessment, which brings us to the third of the myths identified by Coe: teacher assessments cannot be trusted. It is only because of the high-stakes nature of the current testing regime that teachers and schools are forced into 'gaming' when it comes to making judgements about children's capabilities. Remove this, and install a system of cross-checked portfolios, and we have a reliable, thorough and rich picture of what a child can do. As Coe acknowledges, this is a formidable challenge, but the potential results make it one that is worth taking on.

Of the many government interventions to make an impact on educational practice, the promotion of phonics, and in particular synthetic phonics, along with the phonics-check, has been one of the most prominent. Professor Margaret Clark acknowledges that a grasp of phonics can assist some children in learning to read but is adamant that 'the teaching of both reading and writing is most effective when the teaching is systematic, taking into account the linguistic probabilities of the English language and the child's needs'. The overwhelming evidence points to the fact that such practice needs to take place in a real context, not in isolation. When it comes to the phonics check itself, it is costly, time-consuming and, given its importance to a school's ratings, takes up a disproportionate amount of teacher time. As Clark points out, starting the test with 12 pseudo words – *bam, goos, zack, plock* – confuses many children. Teachers' professional judgements and their knowledge of the children in their class takes second place to ensuring successful test results. Children's understanding of what they read is imperilled in this way. With an arbitrary pass mark of 32 out of 40, there is the possibility of the DfE insisting on children retaking the test in subsequent years. As Clark puts it 'the assumption that the needs of those who fail to reach the arbitrary pass mark on this test will still be met by a continuing focus on synthetic phonics as the solution to their problem seems naïve'. Notwithstanding government claims of there being research that substantiates the notion of synthetic phonics being *the* method of teaching reading, Clark's own work reveals that this method is only effective within a broad programme and that using phonics in isolation militates against advancing reading skills, especially when reading for meaning. She is not alone in reaching this conclusion. Oddly, even the government's own commissioned report agrees that 'attainment in reading and writing more broadly appears unaffected by the school's enthusiasm, or not, for systematic synthetic phonics and the check, and by their approach to the teaching of phonics' (Walker *et al.*, 2014: 72).

It seems that officialdom's distaste for expertise extends even to its own documentation.

This predilection for testing rather than learning also extends to mathematics. Primary maths teacher and researcher Gawain Little is critical of a curriculum where there is no emphasis on emphasis, exploration or making links between concepts at the expense of a list of disparate skills to be taught in a disembodied way. He cites Jo Boaler from the Stanford Graduate School of Education who warns about children becoming 'so focused on remembering their different methods, and stacking one new method on top of the next, that they (are) not thinking about the bigger concepts and compressing the mathematics that they (are) learning' (Boaler, 2009: 142). This surface learning is an inevitable consequence of conceptualizing education as a means of producing data and, in an unwelcome twist, turning young people into statistics in what Guy Robert-Holmes and Alice Bradbury from University College London Institute of Education call the 'datafication' of children. They draw on the argument of Ben Williamson from the University of Stirling who suggests that databases reinvent teachers and children 'into data that can be measured and compared, assessed and acted upon' so that these children eventually become 'miniature centres of calculation' (Williamson, 2014: 12). Alpesh Maisuria from the University of East London points to a false application of approaches used in the natural sciences where predictable results are sought from the regularly repeated experiments. This level of certainty, or positivistic logic, is wholly inappropriate when dealing with something as complex and variable as individual children and their approach to learning. Professor Richard Pring captures it neatly when invoking what economists refer to as Goodhart's Law: when a measure becomes a target, it ceases to become a good measure.

This quest for targets results in a curriculum that becomes ever narrower as schools concentrate on achieving test results that will ensure their future and their funding. Professor Pat Thomson from the University of Nottingham points to her research that reveals that nearly a third of state primary schools now only devote an hour a week to art and design. She looks to critical reviews that demonstrate that the arts support children to build a wide range of skills, including leadership, teamwork and taking the initiative. As with so many of her colleagues across the educational research community she points to the fact that the gaps left in the school curriculum as this narrowing takes place are filled by parents with greater income and social capital. A more certain way of reinforcing inequality would be difficult to create.

In March 2013 100 academics published an open letter expressing their concern about the way in which an emphasis on testing was depriving children of the means to learn in a meaningful way that could sustain such learning and be transferable as they progressed through the education system. The response of Michael Gove was to use a right-wing tabloid to label this large group of experts, all of whom have dedicated their working lives to improving the chances of children through education, as the 'enemies of promise'. In commentary that is almost parodic, he expresses the view that:

> You would expect such people to value learning, revere knowledge and dedicate themselves to fighting ignorance. Sadly, they seem more interested in valuing Marxism, revering jargon and fighting excellence.
>
> (Gove, 2013)

Despite this ire from a senior politician who might have looked to such a body for expertise and wisdom, the weight of informed opinion does not support high-stakes testing linked to performance measures. Ideologues such as Gove and his successors are unable to locate research or scholarship to support their own position. It follows, unsurprisingly, that bereft as they are of evidence of their own, they turn on the messengers in an attempt to discredit their work. Schools and school teachers, however, have little doubt about the way in which testing has skewed their working lives and the experience of many children. The chapters that follow, telling the stories of schools who know how to put the test in its place, demonstrate that far from 'fighting excellence', criticizing unnecessary testing and all that goes with it is part and parcel of getting the best out of our young people.

Chapter 5

Trust, values and principles

Still stubbornly hanging around

Among the many developments in schools and education over the past 25 years, the incorporation of vacuous management-speak is one of the least welcome. The nonsensical terminology of service delivery, drilling-down, matrices, indicators and sound data has, somehow, inveigled its way into the language of how we go about the challenging, but enduringly simple, business of getting children to learn how to do things. It is not unusual for school leaders to refer to their 'core business' or, heaven forefend, their 'mission statements' without a hint of embarrassment or any awareness of how silly this sounds. As a consequence, when we consider weighty matters such as trust, values and underlying principles, it can sometimes be hard to take such talk seriously. What united the leaders of all of the schools and settings who agreed to participate in putting together this volume was their openness and willingness to talk about such matters. Furthermore, all school heads and leaders allowed me free access to all areas of their settings and all staff – including non-teaching staff – which afforded the opportunity to see whether practice matched up to rhetoric. I am unapologetic in reiterating a point I make elsewhere in this book; teachers want to talk about their philosophy of education and teaching. More pertinently, they want to know that a set of values genuinely exists in the schools where they work that go beyond feeble, empty aphorisms such as 'every child here knows how to make progress to the next level' or 'here, we respect difference' while stubbornly allocating children to ability sets.

I visit a primary school in the Home Counties that has been at the forefront of the approach of Learning Without Limits (Swann *et al.*, 2012). The visit has not been particularly easy to arrange because of the avalanche of requests the school receives from people from all over the world who wish to see how it operates. On the day I go there is a delegation of around ten education officials from Japan along with a couple of other sundry visitors whose presence is scarcely noted by either staff or children as they go about their purposeful daily business. When I speak to staff about this they all exhibit a cheerful, professional indifference to this wave of visitors of whom they take no immediate notice. They are quick to point out, however, that the children enjoy demonstrating what they know, understand and can do whenever approached by such visitors. The headteacher's work has been publicly honoured and she is about to move to a position of national prominence; government ministers have visited the school and her opinion is sought by them – a situation to which we will return later in the chapter.

In the light of this, what follows may possibly be something of a disappointment for the reader, particularly if the expectation is that there will be an account of innovative, experimental teaching with weird and wonderful goings-on. At face value, what I see is just about as normal and traditional as it is possible to be. It is true that the atmosphere is relaxed and co-operative and that this, of course, does not happen by magic. Children are well organized and self-reliant: they know where to put coats and equipment and they settle into early-morning jobs, routines and activities, all of which speaks highly of a school that has laid out expectations and makes proper demands. I am entertained by a five-year-old who has become intrigued by magic tricks and whose efforts to articulate 'abracadabra' bring a smile to my face every time I recall it during the day. The walls are adorned with displays of gladiators, Halloween, Romans and Egyptians. Year 2 pupils struggle with pictograms and those in Year 6 battle away with metaphors and personification as they work on the beginnings of their story-writing. I admire both teacher and children as they navigate the confusing world of phonics and am proud of myself for keeping up with Year 4's lesson on number sequencing. The teaching is lively and energetic and children do what children do: for the most part they pay attention, occasionally they are diverted from the task in hand and, from time to time, the teacher brings them back in line. It is all just about as conventional as it can be.

There is not even the slightest hint of disrespect in this observation. In fact, I share this with both the headteacher and the teaching staff in our subsequent meetings and they are very gratified by it. To see the essential difference between this school and others we need to wait until the first round of the morning's lessons has been completed.

At the mid-point of the morning, something occurs that is rather different from conventional procedure. The entire school breaks up for 'circle time' during which children from across the age ranges meet together for the sharing of information, the playing of co-operative games and the discussion of whole-school issues. These sessions are led by the children themselves, taking full responsibility for the order and conduct of the meeting, albeit that staff are on hand if needed. They do so with confidence and aplomb and the event is a world away from the usual adult-led assembly. It is testament to, and proof of, a school that says it listens to, values, and trusts its teachers and its young people.

It is this solid foundation of trust upon which the school is built and which marks it out as different. In the subsequent conversation with teachers, one of their number, newly recruited, talks of how a 'cultural confidence' within the school has struck him as its most obvious characteristic. In my earlier conversation with the headteacher, it is this notion of establishing a particular culture that she mentions almost immediately at the start of our conversation. Her comments are littered with references to 'being surprised' by children and of building the agency of teachers and children. There is a fierce determination not to label individuals – either staff or children – or to predetermine their capabilities. She recognizes the customary arranging of children through grading, ranking and testing, and bemoans it as practice that imposes the very limits that her approach sets out to challenge. She despairs of the notion of sound feedback that has deteriorated into the pantomime of coloured pens and feedback-on-feedback that takes place in so many schools. When it comes to formalized testing she is insistent that children take such events seriously and try 'to really show off what they can do': the school's national test results are good and consistent with what might be expected from the intake and statistical projections. They are, however, simply part of the fabric of school life. They do not dominate and it is noticeable, for all its acclaim, that it is not a school plastered with information or excerpts from inspection reports – despite its success in that area.

I ask her where her confidence stems from. She is clear that it has been developed from her own learning and an appreciation of notions of teacher agency – a concept to which she returns on a number of occasions. She points to her own research through her master's degree and her insistence on the school maintaining links with its nearest university. She is adamant that practice at the school be informed by research and evidence and a number of teachers have either gained or are working towards a master's qualification. She tries to foster a genuine interest in pedagogy, as opposed to the pragmatism of practice, wherever possible. The development of teamwork also emerges as a guiding principle.

I meet a large group of teachers from the school separately. I give them no indication of what has been spoken about with the head and ask them what they believe to be the characteristics of the school. Within moments they speak about trust, agency, independence and teamwork. Without giving any impression of having been duped by corporate speak they mention that Learning Without Limits (LWL) is a perfect description of what goes on. 'It's not just about teaching the "stuff"', one of their number explains. 'It's about teaching them to learn. They'll forget the "stuff" pretty quickly. Learning to learn's the important thing.' Once again, the notion of being surprised crops up frequently. They talk of being the sort of teacher they think they'd like to be and of being allowed to go off-course if the occasion demands. In an interesting aside, one of them observes that 'it's not easy being here – you don't get told what to do!' There is appreciative laughter in the room. Their conversation is permeated with references to treating children as individuals and of finding ways to make them flourish.

They are aware that they are not micro-managed – something some of them have experienced in other schools – and talk of being allowed to 'have a go, have a bash'. They are also appreciative of the fact that the data trail and recording and duplication of information that so bedevils the lives of many teachers is something from which they are spared. Like practically every teacher I have interviewed and communicated with during the course of my research in the last seven years, they know that hard work is something they have signed up for and they are grateful that this school asks them to divert their energy into lesson preparation, suitable assessment, and not interminable graph-filling or box ticking. Above all else their commitment to the progress of individual children within the concept of LWL means that they fully embrace the notion of mixed-ability teaching.

It is worth a digression here to explore this idea. If any single approach to the education of children is guaranteed to excite the ire of the political right it is mixed ability teaching – and, on the surface, it is easy to see why. As a young teacher in the 1970s, finding myself in schools that had formerly been grammars and which had undergone what was, in many cases, a reluctant conversion to comprehensive status, I found myself surrounded by teachers for whom setting and streaming were considered the only viable approach to dealing with children operating at different levels. I am at pains to point out that some – by no means all – of these teachers were brilliant at what they did, even when teaching 'lower ability' sets and I learnt a great deal from them. But I equally remember having conversations with them about the value of mixed-ability teaching during which they would arch their eyebrows at me with looks normally reserved for the naïve, deluded and marginally vulnerable. Without being too unkind, their attitude – and that of many such teachers – is summed up in Barry Cunliffe's comment on the Black Papers (Cox and Boyson, 1975) when he writes of how 'teaching difficulties' arise when:

> Trying to get a class of wide IQ range, who have come from 'progressive' primary schools where they have been allowed to

walk around as they please, to sit down and concentrate all at
the same time.

(Cunliffe, 1975: 212)

Twenty years on, Tony Blair, as leader of the opposition, confidently
asserted that:

> The modernization of the comprehensive principle requires that
> all pupils are encouraged to progress as far and as fast as they are
> able. Grouping children by ability can be an important way of
> making that happen.

(In Sukhnandan and Lee, 1998: 44)

Teaching children of the same aptitude in the same place and at the same
pace seems to be nothing more than good, old-fashioned common-sense.
However, as with every instance that attempts to over-simplify the complex,
it's not quite as straightforward as it seems. The notion, for example, of
using IQ as a reliable determinant for academic success – or even as a
viable indicator in itself – has been hotly contested for some time. As for
an understanding of what it actually means to learn something, this, too,
has prompted greater consideration as our understanding of pedagogy and
epistemology has developed. When it comes to the oft-cited concepts of
'pace' and stretching', there is no evidence of any sort to demonstrate that
this happens any better, if at all, in setted situations. The plain fact is that
such evidence that does exist points towards the unsurprising conclusion
that good teaching, rather that grouping arrangements, seems to make
the greatest impact (Major, 2014; Boaler *et al.*, 2000). In this respect the
ongoing work of Professor Becky Francis at Kings (see blogs.kcl.ac.uk/
groupingstudents) is to be greatly welcomed.

There remains a nervousness, particularly in many primary schools,
about communicating these notions of ability to the children themselves.
Hence we have any number of table groupings – bananas and oranges,
reds and greens, lions and giraffes – in an attempt to cloak this; groupings,
incidentally, that are usually completely ineffectual in disguising their place
in the hierarchy from the children themselves, who know exactly why
they're on the strawberry or gorilla table.

The headteacher of the school recognizes the practice and is adamant
that 'if you're a bumble-bee, you'll be in a social mix' but that, broadly,
they avoid 'buttercup and marigold tables'. She expresses concern about
pre-determining what children in the school might be able to achieve and
returns, as she and her staff often do, to the possibility of being 'surprised'

by them. She insists that what she wants to instil is a proper reflexivity in the school where teachers consider why they are doing what they are doing, rather than slavishly following the narrow prescription from elsewhere. She talks of how she wants 'nutritious feeding, not measuring'. She goes on to tell me of how a minibus full of teachers from another school come to visit as an away-day; like me, they see nothing in the day-to-day of the school's operation that is wildly different from a conventional day. 'And they're not going to find anything different,' she tells me, 'until they look into their own hearts' to consider why they approach teaching and learning as they do. She is insistent that she does not 'blame' fellow professionals for behaving in a constrained way, but does heartily wish that her fellow heads would demonstrate more trust and, perhaps, be a little braver.

It is impossible not to be impressed by the head, the teachers, the school, the children themselves, and the all-pervasive atmosphere of optimism. As far as tests being put in their place are concerned, this is definitely the case here; they are acknowledged as important – not least for the children themselves – but they do not dominate. I put a difficult question to the head. Her work and achievements have been acknowledged at the highest level; she has the ear of the great and the good. Her message is one of creativity, positive pedagogy and allowing the whole child to develop. Why, then, do the pronouncements and attitudes coming from central government appear to be at such odds with her outlook? She talks of 'too much political ideology holding sway' and of a profession that 'is not coherent enough to stand up to it'. She bemoans the fact that alongside her own voice, that of a headteacher with unapologetic right-wing credentials and renowned for a 'rod of iron' approach is given an equal (if not more welcome) hearing in the corridors of power. We need, she tells me, to 'go beyond politicians' and to 'show professional courage'.

Her answer is illuminating in a number of ways and the final chapter of this book goes on to consider how to challenge the current hegemony of testing, measurement and scrutiny in detail. For the moment, however, it is important, in terms of what this book sets out to argue, to take issue with this analysis – albeit from a great headteacher in a great school. To argue that 'the profession' can operate separately from political ideology is to try to fight the assault on children and schools with one hand tied behind our collective back. The fact that schools dedicate themselves so thoroughly – if not necessarily enthusiastically – to the production of measurable outcomes can be explained by the way in which education itself has come to be seen as a commodity to be characterized and delivered as a private good or benefit. In many respects, this takes us to the enduring, central question of what is education for? For many teachers – and this has been borne out by my own research – the 'dominance of the old humanist tradition' (Dale, 1989: 129) prevails. Broadly speaking this is based in a belief that education is, in itself, a 'good thing' that works to the benefit of society. This is counter-balanced by the notion of education as producer of human capital, with the state needing and using education as the provider of the skills, knowledge and labour to keep society afloat. To polarize these two concepts, however, is to over-simplify the argument. One would hope that even the most committed liberal humanist would acknowledge the need to enable pupils to operate in the world. Writing as far back as 1961, the critic Raymond Williams warned educators not to fall into the trap of privileging the humanist tradition at the expense of developing 'the absurd defensive reaction that all real learning' is undertaken through this tradition 'without thought of practical advantage' (Williams, 1961: 163).

Nevertheless, in terms of the balance between these two traditions it is plain that over the last 20 years the contention of Friedman and Friedman, the gurus of early neoliberalism, has come to hold sway: 'in schooling, the parents and child are the consumers, the teacher and school administration the producers' (Friedman and Friedman, 1980: 191). It is the conscious adoption of this ideological position by successive governments, both in England and on a global scale, that has led to the ubiquity of a set of conditions characterized by Sahlberg's identification of the Global Education Reform Movement (GERM) (Sahlberg, 2012). Standardization and test-based accountability procedures are the bedrock on which this potion is built and failure to understand that this is not just some temporary brainstorm on the part of politicians who may have temporarily lost their way, is to misunderstand the nature and extent of the balance of forces weighed against any concept of progressive, creative education.

There is a long-standing tradition, albeit one that is fading quickly in an increasingly fragile and insecure world, that politics should be 'kept out of' various parts of life. When I started teaching in 1976 I was given frequent, friendly advice not to drag politics into education (yes, really). We've since heard the same argument applied to various parts of public life – sport and the arts in particular. To believe this is to miss the point and, more crucially, to diminish the possibilities of resistance. As the philosopher Louis Althusser observed, to consider what happens in daily life as somehow separate and removed from political and ideological decisions is an unhelpful stance: 'what … seems to take place outside ideology (to be precise, in the street), in reality takes place in ideology' (Althusser, 1971: 163).

All of which might seem a world away from a wonderful school, swimming against the tide, informed by admirable values and doing a great job with its children. And none of the argument above about how to resist that tide is posited as a criticism of a head and a set of teachers who work tirelessly to put the test in its place. What marks this school out, along with all of those whose work we will look at in the next chapters, is a principled and learned approach to pedagogy and young people. Such places are beacons and examples to us all and that, after all, is the purpose of this book: to demonstrate that such places exist and flourish. How to make an impact on policy and governance will continue to exercise us throughout this volume.

Chapter 6

A state of Grace

Not just about surviving

In the summer of 2015 as part of the research for *Teachers Undefeated* I went on my initial quest to find schools whose headteachers showed a determination to, as I expressed it in that volume, allow the caged birds of their teaching staff to sing. It wasn't an easy search but professional connections eventually led me to two primary schools, one in the heart of metropolitan north London and the other in the Home Counties. When it came to writing up what I experienced in both of these schools, I unapologetically named them as Grace and Hope – much to the amusement of both the staff and headteachers – as an expression of the way in which they were manifestations of these qualities. I did not, and do not, make the claim that these schools are unique and neither do I – or they – believe that they are faultless, but they are different from most institutions and, for the purposes of this particular book, they keep testing firmly in its proper place.

In both instances in 2015 the headteachers gave me access to a group of teaching staff in comfortable surroundings and with a completely free hand to discuss what we wished. This may sound like unnecessarily banal detail, but one of the emergent themes from my researches with teachers is that such space, both metaphorical and literal, has been made unavailable to them as the pace and intensity of school life has increased. In both instances, despite my awareness of the fact that I was prolonging a busy school day, my attempts at closing down conversations with teachers were unsuccessful: they took unbridled delight in talking in a serious and critical way about their beliefs about teaching and pedagogy. And in both instances, when I interviewed the headteachers separately, it was clear to me that these heads had not made any attempt to discover what had been discussed. Just as importantly, the interview with the heads revealed that the beliefs and principles they hoped were at the heart of their schools, were, indeed, reflected in the attitudes and values of their teachers (Berry, 2016; Chapter 7).

All schools believe that they have their own ethos. Someone in my position who has visited hundreds of schools in varying capacities may believe that he is able to pick up something of that ethos, but conclusions can only be partial at the very best. The cynical part of my nature might just observe that any school that feels it necessary to paper its walls with motivational aphorisms or, even worse, reminders that 'in this school we all know which level we're at and how to make progress to the next' might just be revealing more about themselves than they wish. My own research right at the start of my investigations into teacher autonomy also identified an alarming gap between headteachers who were convinced that they were running liberal, autonomous regimes and staff who saw the world somewhat differently. What became clear from conversations with heads and teachers at Grace and Hope was a firm belief in central principles that were needed to guide their daily actions. Of these, the most obvious was trust between colleagues at all levels, as well as trust that children, properly guided, would do the right thing most of the time. From this trust a strong degree of professional autonomy can be developed – and enjoyed – by all. Along with these qualities go a very strong sense of community, underpinned by a commitment to educating the whole child and seeking out talent and ability. Was this strongly expressed ethos in evidence in the cold light of day? In the autumn of 2016 I went to see Grace School in action. I harboured no suspicion whatsoever that I had been duped by the interviews with those who worked there; I just wanted to see what was special about the school. As a researcher and as a teacher I was not disappointed.

The day starts with a conversation with the headteacher, Sam. He is Sam to the parents he greets at the gate, Sam to all of the teaching and non-teaching staff and ... to the children themselves. The school runs on a first-name basis throughout. At this point I can almost see the eyes of some hardened old pros rolling. As this account goes on to reveal, for all of this early indication of informality, there is nothing *laissez-faire* about Grace in terms of conduct or the clear expectations of what the institution requires from all who spend their day there. In a conversation with teaching staff at the end of the day they point to this first-name feature, unprompted, as one of the things that has allowed them to foster good relationships with parents and between staff working at all levels of responsibility. Any potential invitation to cheekiness or over-familiarity from children has long since disappeared as clear ground rules (about, for example the use of diminutives) have become entrenched in the ethos and culture of the school. Having taken on board the news about the use of first-names, the reader will be unsurprised to know that the school has no uniform, which, judging by my journey to the school on public transport and on foot, seems to makes it unique in an area where even tots are decked out in costumes of varying garishness. Children are dressed in the usual unremarkable combinations of polo-shirts, sweaters, shorts and track-pants. There is no fashion show and no ostentation – just kids looking relaxed as they go about the business of doing things and learning.

We walk through breakfast club where it is immediately noticeable that significant responsibility is given to children as they go about looking after their needs and those of others. The school's most recent Ofsted rating was the cherished 'outstanding' but there is no banner on the outside railings proclaiming this and we are spared the usual laminated quotations that so often bedeck the walls of schools that are so favoured. Sam tells me that he is pleased that the school has been judged in this way as it keeps officials off his back, but that 'outstanding is just a thing' and not one that either he or his staff have made any special effort to achieve. In my later conversation with teachers, this is borne out by the comment that they 'couldn't care less' about Ofsted as long as they continue to do the right thing by the children. Sam strolls off to other headteacher duties and I sit down at a breakfast-club table, narrowly escaping a splodge of honey that has found its way on to my seat, to talk to one of the teaching assistants. She tells me that she has worked at the school for more than ten years and that despite having moved from the area she still makes the journey to come to work at Grace. She is, apparently, far from unique in this among support staff and, like most of them, her own children attended the school. This loyalty and longevity of service is something replicated among teaching staff – an issue to which we will return later in this chapter. We are joined by a couple of engaging seven-year-olds who ask me politely who I am and offer me a toasted bagel, and then the school day proper begins.

At the school gate Sam stands, armed with whistle and old-fashioned school bell, and greets parents and children as they arrive. The school population reflects the area, multi-ethnic and multi-lingual, with almost everyone arriving on foot (save for the ubiquitous scooters to be lugged back home by duped parents). Sam exchanges words with as many as he can and then has to stand aside to deal with a parent's concern about a minor incident from the day before. Later Sam tells me that this visibility to parents is central to his *modus operandi* – trying to talk about issues before an interminable email trail is instigated. I repeat a central caveat about this book and its predecessor – there was never a golden age of teaching and education; nonetheless, there is something reassuringly traditional and sensible about this approach to parent-school relationships. Throughout the day all staff talk to me about the school having a definite feel of being a community; there is a good deal of evidence to support this. In a conversation with the person charged with educational pastoral support, this sense of community and an obligation to children that goes beyond the school gates is clear. Her own professional journey from parent volunteer to teaching assistant before gaining qualification as a mentor prior to her current post in charge of this pastoral team is summed up in her observation about the uncharacteristically low turnover of staff and her comment that 'this school means a lot to the community and wider world here'.

Children at Grace behave consistently well. By all accounts, this has not always been the case and, given the difficult circumstances of the lives of some of the children who attend, this is unsurprising. Both the head and staff talk of the regularity with which challenging incidents used to take place and which are now, along with suspensions from the school for misbehaviour, almost unheard of. It is worth digressing from the main narrative here to consider something of the discourse around the behaviour of young people in schools.

The first and most obvious point to make is that nothing, but nothing, about schools and education generates more myth-making than classroom discipline. Things were so much better in the past. I think not. As a grammar school boy from the 1960s, I can give readers my firm assurance that, selected as we were for the development of civil life and progress, if we sniffed even the slightest weakness in any of our teachers, we systematically – and often very ingeniously – set about making their lives a living hell. In later life, as a teacher myself, I am entertained by meeting former pupils who tell me with iron certainty that they wouldn't have got away with half of what youngsters nowadays are allowed to do. The notion that respect and obedience are on a downward spiral is nowhere better captured than in this comment attributed to Socrates from nearly three millennia ago:

> The children now love luxury; they have bad manners, contempt for authority; they show disrespect for elders and love chatter in place of exercise. Children are now tyrants, not the servants of their households. They no longer rise when elders enter the room. They contradict their parents, chatter before company, gobble up dainties at the table, cross their legs, and tyrannize their teachers.

Nonetheless, it would be absurd to suggest that ensuring good order is anything other than a non-negotiable prerequisite for enabling learning to take place. All schoolteachers regard this as a matter of importance. Self-help books for training teachers that deal with pupil behaviour are the first purchased when courses begin; I know as a teacher–educator that the topic of classroom management could take over all seminar sessions if allowed to do so. None of this is remotely surprising. Parents looking at prospective schools want to know the school's reputation for good order. When looking at schools as prospective places of employment, the policies relating to behaviour are often those first sought by applicants. When the DfE document on this states that 'it is vital that the behaviour policy is clear, that it is well understood by staff, parents, and pupils, and that it is consistently applied' (DfE, 2016a: 5) it is stating the obvious. However, the language of this document is revealing in terms of what is an enduringly ideological approach to pupil conduct in schools and one that is deeply rooted in simple notions of behaviourism; readers unfamiliar with this concept might want to look for any reputable website dealing with the works of B.F. Skinner. The terms used in the DfE's 14-page document show that the word 'discipline' appears on 22 occasions, 'power' or 'powers' on 16 and 'punishment' 10. By contrast, 'reward' appears three times and 'learning' only once – and that as a footnote. This emphasis on control is by no means a phenomenon that has only developed in education in a neoliberal age. Nevertheless, it fits perfectly within a system that is characterized by production, outcome, and commodification. Good production systems need to run as smoothly as possible.

I repeat that none of this is part of a call for a soft-edged approach to pupil behaviour; I hope it is not a vain boast to say that any of the thousands of young people I taught in comprehensive schools would vouch for this. The argument here is that the model of discipline and control that has so dominated discourse and practice for so many teachers – and which has been endorsed by many politicians and the popular press – sits uncomfortably with the notion of educating the child in the 21st century. This affection and nostalgia for traditional approaches to controlling behaviour is tellingly captured in the mixed career of Tom Burkard. For some time Burkard enjoyed prominence in the right-wing think-tank, the Centre for Policy Studies (CPS). His most notable achievement was to get this influential body to take seriously his notion of Troops to Teachers as a way of solving difficulties about behaviour in schools. The appeal for some of Burkard's rhetoric is obvious. Ex-servicemen (*sic* – women, apparently, may not demonstrate similar qualities) would 'not be intimidated by adrenaline-fuelled adolescents' because 'unlike most teachers they have been there before' (Burkard, 2008: 13). He goes on to advocate the use of boxing clubs and Christian charities as ways of ensuring good discipline and suggests that 'it would make more sense to encourage motivated servicemen and veterans to attend university than it does to dragoon recalcitrant teenagers into student life' (2008: 19). All of which would be entertainingly comic were it not for the fact that these ideas influenced government thinking and which in their forthrightness are, one suspects, a reflection of prevailing attitudes of those charged with making policy. As a footnote to this episode, the Troops to Teachers programme had only a minimal effect on teacher recruitment and retention (Richardson, 2016). Grace School sees no need for the control and punish approach.

As I observe lessons and sessions during the morning, some children become inattentive and some attempt to distract their companions. They are children; that's their job. When such incidents occur, teachers and other staff consistently and patiently point out to them that they have made wrong choices and suggest other ways of going about their business. Clear alternatives and directions are given; voices are not raised and molehills do not develop into mountains. For the most part, children and adults get on with the business of learning. In my conversation with teachers they tell me that the school has dispensed with stickers and merit points and that they get children to behave well 'because it's the right thing to do'. They have a collective chuckle when telling me that if I had visited very early in the school year, I would have seen 'silent crocodiles' of children as they moved around the school and ground-rules were established, but that this is now a distant memory. One of them observes that they instil notions of care and responsibility as a matter of course and that their actions are interpreted by pupils as 'knowing that we care about them'.

As I make my unaccompanied way around, I observe a visiting orchestra group – whose visits, inevitably, are under threat because of funding cuts – who get children to enact Handel's 'Fireworks Music' with tremendous gusto. Two Year 6 girls enthral me with a story about hunting that they have illustrated with pieces of timber, foliage and debris found in a nearby park and I watch in awe as an energetic teacher drills his Year 3 class to great purpose and with a tremendous sense of fun as they prepare to set about some writing. I wrestle with the ethical dilemmas posed by the story of Icarus and Daedalus in the philosophy lesson and enjoy non-stop cups of 'tea' – consisting of sand – proffered to me in the early years' section by an infant on a bicycle wearing a princess costume. In the hall I am treated to a rumbustious PE lesson where an apparently anarchistic ball game is, it turns out, informed by a clear set of rules and codes of conduct. A sense of purpose and enjoyment is ubiquitous and I am fully aware of the concerted preparation and thought that has gone into these sessions to make them like this: the teachers glide across the surface but their legs are paddling like fury beneath.

What of formal testing and its place in the school? During the course of the morning I meet with a group of seven Year 6 children who are some six months away from taking the national tests prior to moving to the secondary sector. Are these tests important to them, I enquire. My first respondent is adamant that they are: if you do well, she tells me with great earnestness, you get to go on all the bigger rides at Alton Towers at the end-of-year outing. One of her companions is more serious-minded: success in the tests (SATs) means that you get better work once you get to secondary school. Another explains, seriously and methodically, how this is the start of the road to educational success and economic wellbeing. Then, revealingly, one of their number explains that they'll do OK because they'll know what to do and their teachers will remind them when the time comes around. There is a collective nod of agreement. A place exists for the test in the lives of these children and it is neither dismissed nor allowed to dominate.

The issue that does dominate my conversation with these pupils is their recent year-group residential trip. I would like readers to take stock briefly. My visit to Grace took place in October; the school year was barely two weeks old when this trip happened. I ask them whether they had a particular project to attend to and am told that they did not. 'We did team stuff and challenges' and 'we had to learn how to work together and help each other out'. I am informed that they stayed up talking – with *loads* of sweets – until really late but that it didn't matter because all the teachers were down the pub anyway. I note with glee that this piece of folklore about teachers' conduct on school trips persists and when I relay it to staff in my group discussion with them at the end of the day it delights them in equal measure. In more serious vein, teachers tell me how important they consider this trip to be and about the eyebrows it raises with colleagues in other schools. Far from seeing it as a 'wasted week' at the start of SATs year, one of them expresses the view that 'it just seems crazy that you'd put off that sort of experience until later in the year'. They talk of fostering relationships, especially with some children who have previously presented challenges and of how 'you see a different side to lots of them'. They fully recognize that Year 6 is an important year, but in their view so is each school year. As far as SATs are concerned these teachers are resolutely certain that the school 'does not stop for SATs week' by tiptoeing around or making special arrangements and that, in the words of one of them 'if you've taught them well enough, there's no need to wind them up during SATs week'.

Teachers at Grace are not opposed to the use of data. For most of the hundreds of teachers who have spoken to me about data collection, their opposition to it does not stem from an unwillingness to chart a child's progress and attainment but from the frequency and over-detailed nature of the exercise. Grace teachers tell me that they 'take data seriously' and that they have managed to pare back the worst of the box-ticking so that they can use the data to 'see who isn't getting a good enough deal' and try to do something about it. They consider national test results – particularly those in 2016 – as highly unreliable and rely more confidently on their own systems and interpretations. As with headteacher Sam, they are pleased that their 'outstanding' label affords them this degree of freedom but, otherwise, 'couldn't care less' about it. At no time do they quote figures or percentages at me to prove any point. Their job, as they see it, is to ensure that we 'have the best curriculum' and to do the best by their pupils.

Staff turnover at Grace is remarkably low. In a local and national situation where schools increasingly find it difficult to fill vacancies and where new entrants do well to make it to five years' worth of service (DfE, 2016c), this is an exception. I am told variously that 'this is the longest I've ever been in a teaching job' and of the hope that 'this school remains like this'. It is worth making the point that this school is not an 'easy ride' – not that such a thing exists anywhere in the world of education. This is an inner-city, challenging environment. There are a number of factors that keep teachers here. First, there is the sense of trust and community discussed above. Second, hard work is valued and is woven into everything they do: 'it makes it OK to work hard because everyone else is doing it'. The talk is of how they gladly spend time planning good lessons and getting children interested in learning and of how, as teachers, they get energy from this in contrast to the fatigue they know colleagues elsewhere suffer from when 'tick boxing'. Finally, they are well aware of there being another world out there. They swap tales of scripted lessons, planners that have to handed-in days – sometimes weeks – in advance and of displays outside classrooms of 'this week's work' for managers and parents to scrutinize. They are appalled by the lack of trust between school leaders and classroom teachers that can allow such a state of affairs to develop and, once again, contemplate their good fortune in being part of a school where such demands are unknown.

The school chooses to follow the International Primary Curriculum (IPC) (www.greatlearning.com/ipc) and this allows a flexibility and a degree of professional autonomy enjoyed by these teachers. In his seminal works on the ideological provenance of the school curriculum, Michael Apple alerts us to the fundamental notion that in a neoliberal model of education, where outcomes become the most important factor by which all success is judged, much of what we subject our children to is the 'means to reach pre-chosen educational ends' (Apple, 2004: 42). He goes on to explain that:

> In clearer terms, the overt and covert knowledge found within
> school settings, and the principles of selection, organisation

and evaluation of this knowledge, are value-governed selections from a much larger universe of possible knowledge and selection principles.

(Apple, 2004: 43)

A curriculum, and most pertinently a *national* curriculum, is reflective, therefore, of a choice from a range of possibilities. When Sahlberg talks of the standardization of education being one of the principal characteristics of the GERM we can see this enacted in the way that the majority of schools feel constrained to follow a curriculum that is, in its turn, designed to fit the needs of producing a narrow range of measurable outcomes. Why might a school take any chances here, especially if that school is not guaranteed to achieve favourable Ofsted ratings or good test outcomes? Playing safe, however dull that may be, would seem to be the sensible thing to do. Only by developing a genuine ethos – one that goes beyond slogans and epigrams – might a school be able to see that learning and teaching can easily transcend the narrowness of a pre-chosen curriculum and still happily achieve results when they're needed.

As a footnote to my visit to Grace, I have to note that much of it was written up in November 2016 in the aftermath of the election of Donald Trump. For reasons that may not be too difficult to fathom, but which I can't clearly remember consciously thinking about, I found myself revisiting Neil Postman's highly entertaining volume about teaching as a subversive activity and the expression of the belief that 'schools must serve as the principal medium for developing in youth the attitudes and skills of social, political and cultural criticism' (Postman and Weingartner, 1969: 2). As I was contemplating the importance of this concept and of how schools such as Grace have a part to play in this wide, ambitious vision of education, I spotted the following eerie prediction a few pages further on, serving as a warning of what could happen should we fail to produce such critical thinkers:

What we get is an entirely new politics, including the possibility that a major requirement for the holding of political office be prior success as a show-business personality.

(Postman and Weingartner, 1969: 9)

It may seem a long way from a London primary school to the politics of the White House but the ideology of the market is promoted by one and filters through to the other. Resistance to such ideology, at whatever level, is centrally important.

That quiet, but determined, resistance is also in evidence at Hope school that I revisit during the winter of 2017. The geographical setting is different and the school, although ethnically mixed in a way that reflects the composition of the local population, is smaller and rather more homogenous in its composition. In terms of attitude, outlook and values, much of what happens at Grace is mirrored at Hope. Although deemed outstanding by Ofsted, as one enters the school there is nothing to advertise this. Children, although they wear a basic uniform of polo shirts or sweaters, are relaxed and comfortable – and unfailingly polite in an unforced way. Parents chat happily at the school gates, engaging with teaching and non-teaching staff as the day begins.

A full day of observations and conversations has been arranged for me. During a Year 6 maths lesson on turning fractions into percentages I dredge up recollections of how, over half a century ago, I learnt to play with estimating and trialling ways of dealing with numbers and watch on with interest as children work out their own ways of handling this skill. The teacher courteously asks me to explain how I learnt to do this and I just about manage to convey this to the class without too many eyes glazing over. In a Year 4 English lesson we devise the maps and features of the mystery island on which we are going to set our own adventure story: the teacher excites the class's collective imagination with some shared reading and the projection of some startling and stimulating images. In Year 5 we make running rodent music in a session that is, by turns, cacophonous and melodic, but fun and with some real learning at its centre. I watch with genuine interest as another Year 5 class begins to learn the rudiments of programming.

I wish to digress briefly from the narrative of this particular day to say something about the research methodology applied to this book, albeit that a full outline of the details of how data were collected can be found in Chapter 3. My day at Hope was the penultimate visit to a school in terms of the fieldwork undertaken for this piece of work and by this time a theme had clearly emerged frequently in this study: the content and conduct of lessons in these schools is largely unremarkable. Challenging the primacy of testing and scrutiny does not manifest itself in activities that are spectacular in any way. When I put this observation to all school leaders and teachers to whom I spoke, they were happy to regard this as the compliment it was intended to be. The fact that this ordinariness is a feature of all of these schools is worth noting. Methodologically, the assessment of when a qualitative research project has gathered enough data to claim that the concept of 'saturation point' has been achieved remains one that is properly contested (Fusch and Ness, 2015). Nonetheless, I think it can be claimed with some confidence that this ordinariness is very much a feature of the schools who wished to take part in this project – and here it is also proper to acknowledge the principle of purposive or purposeful sampling (Patton, 1990 and see Chapter 3) that has been employed here. These schools took part because they wanted to and felt that they were in tune with the basis of my proposition about putting tests in their place and that, in itself, has a bearing on any sort of claims made by this research. This claim, however, is clear: although informed by principles and values that challenge the hegemonic dominance of high-stakes testing, this opposition does not manifest itself in the bizarre, peculiar or the outlandish but in solid practice that often looks conventional and traditional. There is no quest for silver bullets: just well-planned lessons that – and this is the crucial issue – genuinely put the child's learning at the centre of what takes place.

During the course of the day at Hope I speak to teachers in a range of circumstances. In contrast to what I experience in many schools, almost all teaching staff take a break and eat lunch together in the staff room. I am conscious that as they are doing so they chat, very properly in my opinion, about their pets, the weekend's football, TV and holiday plans: I learn afterwards that 'work talk' has been banned at lunchtime. When I am asked, politely, what I am doing there, the rule is broken. As ever, I am regaled with views and opinions about teaching and education: teachers love to talk about their profession and practice. What emerges from their conversations, unprompted by me, is that they know that this school is different in outlook and approach – and this view is especially pronounced from those who have taught elsewhere. In the arranged interviews with staff and leaders that follow I am given the chance to explore this idea in greater depth.

The most noticeable term that punctuates all conversations is 'trust'. When speaking to a group of teachers at the end of the school day this idea emerges immediately. In a telling comment, one of them observes that 'we're here for reason. We get it and we get children. We don't have to be reminded every minute of the day about what we're supposed to be doing.' They are grateful for the trust afforded them by the school's leaders and for being liberated from the box-ticking. What is more, they believe that this trust is, in its turn, passed on by them to the pupils. One of them grandly explains that 'it's the way we live here' and although there is some good-natured mockery about this, it is a sentiment with which they all express agreement. They want children to 'have a go and do their best' even though they find the requirements of the current curriculum absurd in many ways: 'why,' one of them demands to know with great feeling 'do they need to know what the subjunctive is?' They are determined that their pupils will get the best results possible when it comes to tests, but this will not be allowed to dominate what they do or their attitudes toward learning. One of them expresses this with great eloquence and her comments are worth transcribing in full:

> I don't think we're frightened of the tests, but we're fed up of them. If we took away the SATs, it wouldn't change my attitude and expectations. I'd still prepare, mark and give feedback. I think my teaching would be better because I could stop teaching things that aren't necessary … the tests reduce the children to data.

The comments of these teachers are an echo of the views of their senior managers to whom I speak separately. For them, too, the establishment of trust is the thing about which they speak first and references to it punctuate their comments. There are checks on books, and they do walk around the school, but these regulatory measures are seen as collegiate and developmental interventions by both themselves and the teachers. They are not insistent on cumbersome planning mechanisms and will only pay any attention to this aspect of a teacher's work if they feel that lessons themselves are not going well; one of their number happily admits to the old pro's boast of 'planning on the back of a fag packet'. Above all the senior team sees its work as being built around the notion of putting the child's learning at the centre and trusting to the fact that outcomes will follow naturally as a consequence. I ask whether the school has ever attempted to articulate its guiding principles. The head tells me that, on first being appointed, she attempted to draw up a list of values and then abandoned the notion of doing so because 'actions speak louder than statements of that sort'. Like so many teachers and school leaders to whom I have spoken when researching for this book they talk of the fact that it is not easy working in a school free of pre-determined schemes and rigid templates for assessment. 'We don't care about what colour pen you use to mark some work, it's about the impact it will make on that child.' They key questions, the head and her team inform me, revolve around some very basic considerations: why did we come into teaching, what do we value and how we can eliminate that which is not useful?

A few days after the visit, the head writes to me with some further thoughts.

> As a school we invest heavily in our staff not just in terms of money and resources but we invest in them on a personal level and give them time. We recognise talent and nurture it so both the

children and the staff get a lot out of it. As a result staff commit to the school and stay with us for a long time. Therefore we do not have to keep revisiting our values as we are all very much a part of the journey and growth of the school. We only ever have to induct one or two staff into the school, having already made our ethos and values clear during the appointment process.

This willingness to stay in one school is an echo of the situation described at Grace above. It is worth restating the central importance of the issue of workload when it comes to retaining teachers. This is acknowledged in the latest parliamentary briefing on the issue (Foster, 2017), which builds on work of much recent research in this area. Foster's document is a fair reflection of the circumstances with which anyone acquainted with schools will be familiar. A trawl through 15 pages of text reveals that the term 'unnecessary' relating to workload appears on 14 occasions. This has to be seen against the background of my own research that clearly reveals that it is not *hard* work that deters teachers, but *meaningless* work. The same argument applies to issues about high-stakes accountability, another term mentioned frequently in the report as placing undue pressure on teachers who have no problem with the notion of being answerable whatsoever. I turn to the research of the last seven years during which I have taken evidence from nearly 150 teachers who tell me that they have plenty to offer children and will gladly do so, irrespective of the amount of work that entails. What drains, discourages and exhausts them is the meaningless, unnecessary recording and reporting and the apparatus that needs to be put in place, which attempts to reduce the tricky, messy business of learning to a single integer to be tabulated in set of outcomes. In Grace and Hope teachers are afforded that space in settings that are genuinely driven by principles and values: the whole child comes first, assessment is important, but learning takes pride of place.

Chapter 7

More than a grade
Loving the subject at secondary level

And still they gaz'd and still the wonder grew
That one small head could carry all he knew.
('The Village Schoolmaster' by Oliver Goldsmith,
18th-century poet)

There is a pervasive idea sutured into the English education system that every stage of a child's progress is nothing more than preparation for the next one. This often manifests itself in a view that although a degree of experimentation and freedom may be all well and good at primary level – albeit that successive governments have done their best to ensure that as much prescription as possible is applied there as well – when it comes to the serious business of secondary school, conformity and adherence to examination demands must dictate proceedings. While planning this book and looking for potential schools to participate, colleagues and fellow professionals often observed that it might prove difficult to find such secondary schools in the current climate of accountability and public scrutiny. I was grateful and relieved when, through contacting networks and individuals, I was able to identify a number of such schools and, most importantly, three who were willing to invite me to observe lessons and other activities as well as giving me time and space to speak to teachers.

On a foggy, frosty morning in November 2016 I arrive at one such school on the fringes of a city in the east of England. Unbeknown to us all, the world will experience the shock of Donald Trump's election the next day and it is encouraging to see and hear that throughout the day whenever the subject is raised by young people – often in the crude and binary way reflective of the discourse around both Trump and Brexit – teachers are content to let the issue run and to participate and steer conversations where appropriate. This relaxation about going 'off-script' is an early indication of the values and ethos that inform how the school operates.

Having grown accustomed to the almost mandatory banners that adorn school gates and entrances informing visitors of the current Ofsted status of the institution, I am entertained by a simple greeting over the door that welcomes visitors using the affectionate soubriquet of the school, used, as I find out during the day, by all staff and students. The school is a reflection of its local area in terms of a broadly middle-class intake; it has resisted the drive to become an academy and has remained under local authority control. Its examination results are above national average, although not by any huge margin, and the school, reflective of the local area, is largely mono-ethnic. I will be meeting members of the humanities department who have collectively expressed an interest in sharing their practice with an outside researcher. I begin the day with a conversation with the headteacher.

We start by her asking me how I found my way into higher education (HE) from my previous life as a schoolteacher and from there we move on to her telling me about a recent meeting with educationalists from her local HE institution – dubbed in the world of the education market as a 'provider'. She expresses disappointment at the fact that, as she sees it, the university now sees itself as something of a servicing institution. It sees its job as to note the trends and priorities of central government in relation to teacher education and the provision of professional development and then to frame its relationships with local schools accordingly. We both acknowledge a degree of understandable pragmatism about such an approach, but bemoan the lack of intellectual challenge in the adoption of this degree of survivalism (Ball, 2008). She is particularly disappointed – as am I – about an approach to the continuing professional development (CPD) of teachers and school leaders that does little more than examine ways of acquiring higher Ofsted ratings – the ubiquitous 'from good to outstanding'. Her own view of what CPD should facilitate is a means of allowing teachers a degree of reflexivity about their practice, sometimes with formal accreditation but at other times just for its own sake. In my meeting with teachers later in the day, I see ample evidence of this approach in action.

The head is adamant that her leadership is informed by clear principles and a set of values that she shares with colleagues at all times. I need here to be precise in how I express the following observation: whenever I interview headteachers they always say this. I am not suggesting for a moment that by doing so any of them are liars or charlatans, although some may push that boundary closer than others. What I am saying is that the enactment of such a principle may sometimes be more honoured in the breach than the observance. I shall explain what has led me to this conclusion.

The drive towards academization of schools in England prompted widespread opposition at local and national level. I actively participated in such opposition at a number of levels: as a trade-unionist, a teacher, later as a teacher-educator, and also as a parent. At a local level I was known to many heads, the teachers in their schools, and many members of governing bodies.

In various capacities I would attend the sparsely attended 'consultation' meetings at which the case for conversion to an academy was put from the top table and I would be a vociferous opponent of this when given the chance to speak from the floor. In almost all cases such opposition to conversion failed, but it was what happened as such meetings broke up that was illuminating. Headteachers and other senior figures (one of whom I had taught at school) would quietly approach me and tell me that, actually, they agreed with me and didn't want to convert to an academy, but, well, you know how it is ... financial incentives, middle-class parental pressure, the promise of independence. There were often a difficult few moments when I would have to point out to them that if they were genuinely opposed to the process then the proper thing to do would be to say so and act accordingly. Given this propensity to moral timidity on the part of some school leaders, I have learnt to treat expressions of high principle with some caution.

The head tells me that she would rather have a school that was open-minded and even on occasion experimental in approach than one that, in her words, 'chases "outstanding" like all of the local academies'. She tells me that she has worked hard to gain the support of the parental body and the governors. She acknowledges that the school's profile in terms of examination results allows her a degree of leeway and that although everyone strives to ensure that all children gain as many good qualifications as possible, it is something about which they remain relatively relaxed. Later in the day she explains that headship is not something for which she had planned but that circumstances had brought her to this position and it is now her 'life's work' to lead the school well. She gives up her office at lunchtime so that teachers can talk to me collectively and when she asks them whether she should leave so that they can talk more freely, they are entirely adamant that she should not do so.

The school day begins with an assembly on the theme of Armistice Day and the events leading up to it. It is conducted in way that clearly provokes thought from the students, who are also appreciative of a commemorative song written and performed with some aplomb by two Year 11 pupils. Proceedings are orderly throughout and at the end chairs are cleared with no fuss and little noise. I draw attention to this seemingly banal situation for one important reason: other examples of how a simple assembly on an important theme, that any outsider might consider immune from disruption, are readily available. Many schools are bedecked with laminated aphorisms about respect, good conduct, and the treatment of other people, none of which is evident when observing the day-to-day churn of school life. When such conduct is apparent, it is too easy to fail to recognize the unrelenting work that goes towards establishing such an atmosphere.

I move on to a history lesson in Year 9. There is much Trump/Clinton chatter among the pupils as they enter the room; 'Sir' is asked for an opinion that he duly delivers along with a couple of pithy reasons and the lesson begins. I had been insistent that nothing special be laid on and what I see is a genuine, workaday lesson. A marked assignment on the previous topic – the French Revolution – is handed back and we are to carry on with recently started work on the suffragette movement in Britain. The return of the assignment, which I later discuss with the teacher at some length, is worthy of some detailed description and discussion.

The school has made two far-reaching policy decisions. The first of these is that all subjects are taught in mixed-ability groupings; setting and streaming are things of the past. Second, formal marks, grades, and levels are no longer awarded: the teacher ticks parts of the work that are done well and writes formative comments. As the teacher and I observe with some laughter in our subsequent conversation, this land free of harsh judgements does not stop kids, in the time-honoured way, from looking over at their friends' work and asking 'how many ticks didya get?' The next part of the process is for students to look at the teacher's comments and marry them up with a grid of success criteria pasted into the front of their exercise books. The teacher does not check on this process as such but moves around the room, commenting on what each child has done and answering questions – genuine questions – about the French Revolution as well as prompting some speculative thought from some of them. To make the point unequivocally, the children are interested in the French Revolution and when the lesson moves on to the current topic it is equally clear that most of them are very interested in the suffragette movement. There is much entertaining speculation about the evidence pertaining to Emily Davison's intentions on Derby Day in 1913. What they are not interested in is matching up Sir's comments to the success criteria and they approach this task, for the most part, in a decidedly desultory way.

At the end of the lesson we chat in a collegiate way. I compliment the teacher on, as far as I can see, communicating his obvious love of subject to the students and how this has made the lesson a pleasure to observe. He chooses to talk to me about the assessment process and about how it has taken him, a teacher with ten years' experience, some time to 'wean myself off' the giving of grades, although he is now entirely committed to this new way of operating. Then, entirely unprompted, he expresses the concern that even with grades stripped out of the process, the 'matching' exercise could, in its way, simply be another way of accommodating teaching that could be dominated by the meeting of assessment objectives. I hesitate before expressing the view that this is exactly what it could become, but that the very fact that he had recognized this potential danger means that he will probably guard against it. I am unable to judge whether what follows is a spontaneous decision or one prompted by my presence to reflect on his practice, but we finish our conversation with his expressing clear determination to 'go the whole hog and get rid of that grid too'. I leave the reader to consider the metaphorical association between grids and cages.

In the Year 10 geography lesson that follows there is an interesting balance achieved between the needs of fulfilling the requirements of a public examination and the obvious commitment on the part of the teacher to get children to love the subject. They have just returned from the woods that fringe the playing field armed with clipboards, results and observations. Lest the reader think that this is some sort of idyllic establishment peopled only by serious-minded and committed students, I had caught glimpses of them out there during the previous lesson and had seen all of the regulation mucking about and horseplay associated with release from the classroom. Nevertheless, the class settles happily into its work looking at local eco-systems and showing quiet appreciation of the teacher's efforts in setting up the whole enterprise. He allows himself a brief digression to talk about mammal traps and to illustrate these with a YouTube clip; both he and the class are happily diverted. As in the previous lesson, one of the characteristics of this session is a willingness on the part of students to ask questions unprompted. The fairest assessment of what is happening is that the teacher is properly enthusiastic and energetic and his class is happy enough to play along with this. I reiterate a point made above: this may seem unremarkable but is a situation teachers have to work very hard to achieve.

For it all, there will be a test at the end of the topic. The students are aware of this and occasional reference is made to it. What is more, work and spoken contributions of a high quality are awarded with house points, with the added incentive of future 'prom passport points' for effort and achievement. There is a strict rota for individual feedback sessions on the work leading to the test and the regulations around this are firm and non-negotiable: sign-up for your session or miss the opportunity. I mention all of these issues to emphasize the point that this not a free-for-all environment liberated from the demands and expectations of a highly regulated and carefully scrutinized system of schooling. What is clear, however, is that these needs are accommodated and do not dictate the terms of the lessons or, indeed, all of its content. In a later conversation with this teacher he tells me that although he is relatively inexperienced, he appreciates learning his trade in an atmosphere in which the prevailing attitude is one where flexible and interesting teaching will lead to good test and exam results. He knows, as do the colleagues with whom I speak during the break that follows, that this confident approach is relatively rare in secondary schools. When I talk to a small group of teachers over coffee they are acutely aware of the need to balance engagement with subject matter, even allowing themselves to stray from the focus from time to time, with the need to equip students to deal with the demands of the assessment regime.

As I walk to the next lesson the teacher is slightly apologetic. This will not be exciting, I am told: we are planning a formal essay about the Battle of Hastings with Year 7. It is true that this is not a lesson characterized by lively group work, role play, or enactments of arrows entering the eyes of unfortunate monarchs. But what becomes clear as we go through the lesson is that all of these things have occurred beforehand and have made an impression on the class. They know and understand a good deal about the Battle of Hastings, its strategic importance, and some of the military tactics used. They do so because they have spent time on the field being opposing armies and time in class debating the relative merits of infantry and archers. In other words, the engaging and exciting work has been done beforehand and this teacher is able to strike the deal made by all good teachers: we'll do plenty of exciting stuff but, from time to time we need to formalize our learning. This very traditional lesson about how to write a formal essay is deftly handled – and done without a learning objective or assessment focus in sight. What is noticeable is that the teacher has understood that it is not necessary to be constantly telling children what they are doing and why. This often occurs in lessons because of a misunderstanding that this is 'good practice' and 'what Ofsted wants'. The opposite is true. In its own words, Ofsted counsels against such an approach:

> In lessons observed, significant periods of time were spent by teachers on getting pupils to articulate their learning, even where this limited their time to complete activities and thereby interrupted their learning!
>
> (Ofsted, 2012: 14)

We push on and draft our first paragraph; we stop for the occasional joke or brief question and answer and this formal, traditional lesson takes its course. Assessment is important, but firmly in its proper place.

During the lunch break I meet with half a dozen teachers and the head. I express my gratitude to them for giving up precious time in the middle of the working day, and from that point onwards I say very little for the next 40 minutes. I make the point elsewhere in this book and in *Teachers Undefeated* that one of the most damning indictments of the speeding up of the school day is that it has closed down all sorts of opportunities for teachers to discuss their practice. I make no apology for reiterating the point and for condemning this development: I would challenge anyone who doubted the importance of allowing such open discussion to listen to the recording of this particular conversation.

In a wide-ranging exchange we cover topics such as the balance to be found between the teaching of skills and subject knowledge; in a complex exchange of views the primacy of Bloom's taxonomy and the way in which it is sometimes crudely applied is challenged. There is consideration of the ideological drive behind curriculum content, particularly in humanities subjects; there are mixed views about the effectiveness of the stripping away of grades balanced against children's entitlement and need to know how they are doing. What is the place for genuine student voice in these matters; do students have a proper right to see how they're doing in relation to their peers? In all of this I am an interested non-participant as professionals discuss the serious business of teaching and learning in a collegiate and informed way. I am in the company of dedicated, highly skilled and knowledgeable practitioners who, like so many of their colleagues whose views I garner as part of my research, express frustration and disappointment towards a government that it considers out of touch with the needs and development of young people. They are fully aware of the need to be accountable to students and their parents and they embrace this responsibility willingly. They are not looking for an easy life.

They recognize that not all schools are like this one. 'We're lucky to work in a school where we're not hauled over the coals if things don't go quite as we anticipated,' says one. 'I'll teach a particular topic the best way I can and get them to like it – the results will come, the exam will be OK,' says another. I reiterate a point made above: this is not school and teacher paradise. They bemoan the way that even at this early stage of the school year some students are slumped and indifferent, driven only by the perennial, unchanging mantra – 'will there be a test on this – is it in the exam?' These teachers know they have some way to go before the principles and ethos that drive them are fully taken on board and universally adopted by all of their students. What is abundantly clear from this conversation, however, is that principles and values do inform their actions in a way that goes beyond merely satisfying a data collection process.

During the rest of the day I see a Year 9 class grappling with the notion of different models of industry and, in the course of doing so, begin to understand something of the notion of globalization. I watch a Year 11 teacher in the last lesson of the day bravely take on the notion of whether or not Donald Trump genuinely espouses Christian values with particular reference to immigration and in doing so, by her own cheerful admission, spend a good 40 minutes making the extraction of blood from a stone look relatively straightforward by comparison. In both lessons the ability of teachers to think on their feet, adapt to the response and reactions of their classes, and to bring the real world into the classroom are obvious. There is no script to be followed, no slavish writing down of learning objectives, and not an assessment criterion in sight. They are trying to enable students to understand concepts and ideas.

My conversation with the Year 11 teacher is companionable and good-natured as I both commend her on taking on something of such great relevance and, in turn, commiserate with her on the way in which, apart from some worthy stalwarts, few of the class openly responded to the topic. Yet there is something here about knowing how people learn and it is a world away from the crude, linear model espoused by governments frantic to demonstrate that learning has taken place and progress has been made. Pam Jarvis (2016) makes this obvious point but one that should be inscribed on the heart of all of those desperate to know 'what was learnt in this lesson':

> Human beings need time to absorb ideas, and to apply them in many different ways, most crucially being given the latitude to do this in some ways that succeed and in some ways that don't.
>
> (Jarvis, 2016)

It is not a stretch of the imagination to believe that a student who had sat quietly during the lesson on the day before Trump was elected may have made something of a connection between what happened in the last lesson of a tiring school day and the events in the real world as subsequent events unfolded. Training teachers are taught about constructivism – albeit rather too fleetingly in many cases – and yet much of what happens in school seems to demand that evidence of learning is immediate and predictable. With more than a century of modern pedagogical study at our disposal, this rather dismissive model of how education works is dispiriting. Fortunately, teachers at this school are better informed and temper their professional actions accordingly. Above all, what is clear when talking to these teachers and watching them in action is a deep interest in, even a love of what they are teaching.

There is a need for some authorial caution here. I have never argued that there was a golden age of teaching or teacher autonomy and, by the same measure, there was never a world of schools populated by practitioners whose every move was informed by a love of their subject. Yet it is clear that the requirements for being an *effective* teacher – a telling description in itself – has altered over the last 30 years since the introduction of the National Curriculum and its associated demands. Writing in 1999, Ball observes pessimistically that:

> It is difficult not to conclude that political enthusiasm for accountability and competition are threatening both to destroy the meaningfulness of 'authentic' teaching and profoundly change what it means 'to teach' and to be a teacher. The global trends of school improvement and effectiveness, performativity and management are working together to eliminate emotion and desire from teaching – rendering the teachers' soul transparent but empty.
>
> (Ball, 1999: 9)

In the same year, the work of Davies and Edwards led them to the conclusion that teaching was in danger of becoming 'a techno-rational activity, the underlying mechanics of which can be ... universally applied in the classroom' (Davies and Edwards, 1999: 269). To deepen the gloom, when one searches for academic articles relating to the importance of subject knowledge for teaching, apart from some work relating solely to mathematics, investigation into the topic runs out in about the middle of the 1990s. Along with a good deal of anecdotal observation, often from older teachers, there does seem to be some justification for believing that subject knowledge has taken a back seat in an age of performativity and measurable results. Indeed, I was jarred into research myself by the dispiriting revelation that there were English teachers out there who didn't read for pleasure and for whom the teaching of whole texts had become something belonging to a distant age. The more encouraging outcome from that research (Berry, 2016) is the clear message that for many teachers, the enthusiasm for what Ball calls 'authentic' teaching has not been killed off – just subdued by circumstance.

Some weeks later I visit another secondary school. In 2001, Tony Blair's official spokesman Alistair Campbell talked of his concern over what he dubbed 'bog standard comprehensives' (Clare and Jones, 2001).

He intended this as a term of disapproval but many schools and teachers were happy enough to adopt it for themselves as a description of a decent school in ordinary surroundings doing its level best for the students it had. All of which is by way of saying that I visit a bog standard comprehensive in an outer London borough, serving a relatively mixed community in a geographical area that is neither deprived nor noticeably affluent. I immediately feel at home in surroundings familiar to me during the majority of my school teaching career. Yet certain things do mark this school out as different. As with the school described in the first part of this chapter, there is a willingness to engage with pedagogic ideas and to encourage teaching based on the choice of material that is engaging, relevant, and which above all teachers themselves feel free to interpret and develop in an individual way.

I am greeted by the head of English in whose department I will be spending the morning. She tells me something of the recent history of the school – which has not been easy. Having veered close to Ofsted disapproval ratings, a new management team was installed. The usual reaction of schools to this situation is to impose regimes of tight scrutiny of teachers' actions, reductive curricula and demanding systems of data collection (Case *et al.*, 2000; Perryman, 2006). This school opted for a very different route. A new head and senior management team worked with teaching staff to introduce mixed-ability teaching across the board. A marking policy based on formative comments with no grades or numerical assignations was adopted. Lessons were to be planned according to the needs of students with, as one teacher explains to me 'no need to use those horrible frameworks'. One teacher explains it aptly, 'we held our nerve' and another, somewhat more bluntly, says that it was a way of saying 'up yours' to those whose reactions to such difficulties would be to retreat into narrowness and timidity. The school bases much of its professional development around the work of Carol Dweck and the notion of growth mindsets, using its intranet to post 'think pieces' that form the basis of group meetings. Much of this development is aimed at 'helping kids manage connections across things' – and staff are encouraged to engage in research into informed practice to this end as a matter of course. There are doubters: it has taken time to convince all teachers of the viability of mixed-ability teaching and not every member of staff buys into the idea of being a teacher–researcher. However, what is clear from these early conversations, and what becomes even clearer as I observe the actions of teachers and students, is that this is a school that runs on values not slogans – something characteristic of all schools that put the test in its proper place.

The first lesson I see is with a Year 9 class reading John Steinbeck's *Of Mice and Men*. This short but dense text was ubiquitous on examination syllabi until it emerged that it irked Michael Gove who had it removed (Kennedy, 2014). As a teacher, I loved the text for dozens of reasons, not least the opportunity to imagine the voices of the main characters and to read them to my classes who, depending on circumstance, would try their own versions. It was called 'bringing a text to life'; Hector in the *History Boys* (see Chapter 1) would have approved even if Mr Gove did not. If I did not hear a few sobs when we read the ending together, I would feel that I had been derelict in my duty. I am delighted to be in the company of a young, dynamic teacher who is cut from the same cloth. With no 'starter' activity and with no lesson objective on the board, we plunge into a free-flowing recap of where we are in the story as she furiously jots down the class's ideas on an old-fashioned whiteboard. What becomes clear is that they know and like this text: we discuss the hierarchy of the oppressed individuals; we read aloud with expression and laughter; we do not avoid tricky issues, particularly about race; we make a few notes before we finish and depart happily for the next lesson.

I move to a Year 10 class looking at bias in language. To use the well-worn teachers' euphemism, this class is 'lively', albeit in an entirely non-malicious way, but they fuss, fidget, nudge and stretch – because they're 14 years old. The very positive side of this is that they are bursting with ideas and are determined that others will hear what they have to say. The teacher handles it all brilliantly. With contemporary examples of language in public use about immigrants, Brexit and the 'dumping' locally of a body, we examine how language is carefully chosen in order to sway and manipulate audiences. It is clear that there is a range of understanding in this mixed-ability class, but there is no obvious disengagement – far from it – and there are comments and observations of the highest order from some students. It neither looks nor sounds neat and tidy, but that does not mean that it is disorderly in any way: learning is a messy, non-linear business and this lesson bears that out entirely. This is a school where, in common with practically all others, there are book trawls and 'learning walks', albeit not so named here. However, in conversation with this teacher and her colleagues, these devices are seen as collegiate and helpful rather than threatening. The making of occasional mistakes or lessons, like this one, that can sometimes stray off course, are accepted as part of a wider pattern that looks at learning as a process, not the sum of a linear series of delivered lessons.

In Year 11, on the day that the BBC announces its candidates for Sports Personality of the Year, students are shown a short promotional film before discussing who they would choose prior to embarking on planning a short speech to support their chosen individual. As with so much that I witness at both schools, this willingness on the part of teachers to prepare and present work that is immediate and relevant is a salient characteristic. To echo the words of one of the primary teachers interviewed in Chapter 5, doing such work is not easy. There are no pre-prepared lessons on Brexit, Trump, or even a sporting award. Publishing companies eager to make money on the need for quick, replicable lessons cannot cater for the needs of young people in the way that a teacher, who is prepared to put in the extra hours to bring this immediacy to the classroom, is able to do.

When I speak to teachers collectively during their lunch break they reaffirm the need for them to be given the confidence to follow their educational instincts in this way. Many of them talk of having experienced assessment-led teaching elsewhere and invoke systems where written work had to be produced every lesson – to show that 'work' was being done – and of draconian scripts and procedures to be followed in every lesson. In an echo of so many comments from teachers I have spoken to in the last seven years of my research, they bemoan the fact that they have were in danger of becoming functional teachers, capable of generating results and outcomes but having forgotten the inherent interest and excitement that should have been central to what they were actually teaching. They know that they have some way to go but are encouraged by the fact that examination results hold up well, giving them leeway to teach as they do. 'We're not out of the tunnel,' says one, 'but we're getting there and it's much better than just ticking stuff off to say that it's done.' They show particular interest in the topic of this book and send me away with a friendly instruction to get them as many examples as possible of schools who are prepared to trust their pedagogical instincts in the same way as they are.

My final visit to a secondary school is an oddity. A long-standing colleague, whose opinion I value highly, tells me of a professional visit he has made recently to a school. When he names it, I express scepticism about its use in my research. It is a state school in the Home Counties, although my own ignorance is exposed when I admit that I had thought it to be a private establishment. A visit, first to its website and eventually in person, might excuse my presumption. Solid Edwardian buildings, manicured lawns and many of the trappings of the English public school are in evidence – albeit that a short venture beyond these façades takes one to the comfortable territory of ordinary scruffy and stuffy classrooms. Although a state school, there are some children who are boarders and the school week extends into Saturday morning. The official position is that it is not a selective establishment, but practically everyone I speak to recognizes that, de facto, this is the case, especially with the emphasis given by the school to the teaching and learning of languages. For those students – the vast majority – who stay on past the age of 16, the school bases its studies on the International Baccalaureate (IB) and for those between 11 and 16, it uses the IB Middle Years Programme (MYP). The IB is studied by fewer than 200 schools in England and almost all of these are in the private sector. Its principal features are that, through the choice of six subject areas, students will explore what it is to learn, ask challenging and thoughtful questions, develop a sense of culture and identity and learn to communicate with people from different cultures and countries. The guiding principle of MYP is that students are urged to make practical connections between their studies and the real world. The school does enter students for GCSE examinations at 16 although there is not the clamour to rack up as many successes as possible as one encounters elsewhere. Some subjects are taught in languages other than English. The reader, like me, is entitled to think that this is not the 'real world' of children and schools: I would not dispute this, but would argue that there is still something to be learned from such an establishment.

When I contact the school to arrange a visit, a senior member of staff tells me that they welcome such events and are always looking for comment from informed observers. I am encouraged by this and look forward to the very full and varied day that has been carefully planned for me. Once again I am given free rein around the school, epitomized by a start to the day when I am granted an unsupervised interview with two sixth formers. They are both fulsome in their praise for the amount of support that is given, both in terms of their demanding academic studies and their extra-curricular interests. They talk openly about the care that they feel staff take over them and of the fact that they genuinely feel that their happiness as students is taken into consideration by those at the top of the school and the head in particular. They acknowledge that they are 'very lucky' and that the school is not 'an exam factory, which is all the school cares about'. It is not, however, an unsullied landscape of loveliness. One of them admits that in the run-up to GCSEs she 'lost my passion' for learning and was surprised by instructions from some teachers to stop reading around subjects – something she had previously enjoyed – in case 'it all became confusing'. When I ask her how long this lasted for, she tells me that it may have been half a year but that, thank goodness, her passion has returned. I forbear to tell her that a mere half-year sounds like small fry in comparison to the coaching and drilling endured by her counterparts elsewhere.

During the course of the morning I speak to senior members of staff and have an individual interview with the head. The senior teachers tell me that having experienced teaching in an IB school they would not go elsewhere – although my old-timer's eye tells me that they are being overly modest in an attempt to emphasize the advantages of the IB. They, like the headteacher in the subsequent discussion, acknowledge that there are tensions in the school year and that Year 11 'suffer the same boredom' as they might do in any school. What is common to all of our conversations, however, is an insistence that the school's practice is informed by values. They articulate the notion that good subject teaching is the *sine qua non* of their approach and they trust to the fact that results will follow as a consequence. 'If you teach well and follow a good curriculum, exam results come as a by-product,' the head tells me. I am told that idiosyncratic approaches from teachers are encouraged and enjoyed by all and that no need is seen for lesson templates or pre-designated instructions or routines. Teachers are expected to work hard and in turn are trusted to get on in their own way. This trust also extends to self-directed professional development where teachers are given an allocation of time to pursue their particular interests.

As with all such commentary from school leaders, it is instructive to attempt a degree of triangulation when talking to teaching staff. In unplanned, casual conversations with teachers during the day this very positive picture is broadly confirmed. There is a clear recognition that the school is a principled, value-driven institution, albeit a privileged one, and that in comparison to many teaching colleagues elsewhere they are afforded a degree of autonomy and trust that is greatly appreciated. Teachers do not doubt that the message to teach creatively is one that they hear on a regular basis and they do not appear to doubt the sincerity of the exhortation to do so. To imagine, however, that they are free from the stress of generating the results that remain important for the institution's profile would be to miss the point. Two principal issues emerge from my discussion with them. First, the comment that 'targets and grade generation are still here' typifies a number of conversations I have: the general paraphernalia of data collection may be lighter in touch than some of them have experienced, but it is still there. Second, to borrow the phrase from Storey (2009) there is evidence of an 'earned autonomy' from teachers: creativity may have to be earned once results are guaranteed – which is at odds with the 'good results follow good teaching' mantra. One teacher tells me, without rancour, that 'I don't think we're as exceptional as we think we are'. When it comes to professional development, I am told that an attempt to establish a research community in the school, although not obstructed by school leaders in any way whatsoever, is something of an uphill struggle. The senior teacher charged with overseeing innovative practice bemoans the fact that younger teachers have limited horizons in how they view the profession ... although I direct her, of course, to *Teachers Undefeated*, which challenges such conclusions.

None of which is to undermine the greater vision of a school that does, for the main part, set its sights higher than the gaining of examination success. As with all my visits to schools, I see a selection of engaging and interesting lessons including, on this occasion, a Japanese lesson with Years 12 and 13. I am intrigued, almost comforted, to note that although the language itself is different, exotic even, when it comes to understanding irregular verbs, there is no way round it other than repetition, chanting and establishing whatever pattern works for the learner. In a Year 10 history lesson I enjoy the engaged banter of a class that likes both the subject and the teacher. I am appalled, though, along with the teacher, at a crammed, mechanical syllabus that seems specifically designed to squeeze the life out of the subject by reducing the topic of wounded World War I soldiers to a dry list of the exact procedure for assigning treatment. As ever I see no bells and whistles, no outlandish or experimental practice: the quality is in the pedagogy and thoughtful practice that lies behind the activities.

All three of these schools attempt to mitigate the worst excesses of a system that demands good results as its central criterion for success. None of them suggests that the acquisition of these results are not important, they just try not to let the test dominate. To whatever extent we believe their efforts successful, what they are doing, consciously or not, is swimming against an ideological tide. They are attempting to privilege pedagogy over practice and in doing so they are tackling a historical problem endemic to the English education system. In 1981 Brian Simon wrote a seminal essay bemoaning the lack of pedagogical knowledge in teaching and the training of teachers in England (Simon, 1994) and it is a text to which educators and critics have frequently returned. In both 2004 and 2010 his friend and colleague, Robin Alexander, who was once one of the loudest voices in the ear of policy makers, revisited his work to regret that little had changed (Alexander, 2004 and 2011). Alexander is impatient with policy that, as he sees it, revisits exhausted arguments about the primacy of skills as opposed to subjects, culminating in 'the ultimate pedagogical nonsense' (2011: 3) of an imagined division between teaching and learning. The target of his irritation may well have been a figure like Michael Barber, a self-styled education 'guru' who, tellingly, has the keen attention of policy makers around the world with his notion of 'deliverology' (Barber *et al.*, 2011). At the bottom of such an approach is the apparently commonsensical notion that 'what works' is all that counts. What such an approach doesn't do is to ask 'what works for whom – and for what purpose?'

I return to one of my commonly used anecdotal themes to illustrate the point here. Conversations with former pupils take many forms. A frequent formula, however, is captured here. On chance meetings an ex-pupil will jokingly say something like 'I don't know how you got me through GCSE English, but I'm very glad you did!' before dredging their memory to recall a text (often, I'm delighted to report, Shakespeare) that they surprised themselves by enjoying. And that will be that. They have seen themselves through life with a basic, necessary qualification – tick – and have remembered something they enjoyed doing – tick. Quite how the apparatus of a market-led, commodified, GERM-ridden system has made this apparently simple business so cumbersome and potentially soul-destroying should vex us all.

Chapter 8
A jewel shining in the gloom
What a school can do when principles take centre stage

My final visit takes me to vibrant school in a challenged community. It is impossible to talk about what happens here without painting something of a picture of the environment in which it operates.

The school is located in an area of the country once dominated by coal mining and the associated trades and occupations that supported that industry. The effect of the failure of reinvestment in such communities is widely recognized and well documented (Foden *et al.*, 2014). Levels of unemployment, ill health, low life expectancy, and youth unemployment still blight such areas some 30 years after the British state ensured the end of coal mining as a viable means of energy production. According to the work of Foden and his colleagues, 43 per cent of former mining communities fall into the worst 30 per cent of areas of social deprivation. The school itself is situated in an area that, according to the government's indices of multiple deprivation, places it in the top 18 per cent of disadvantaged boroughs (DCLG, 2015). Tucked away as a beacon of brightness in a drab area of town, the school is clearly fighting against the odds. The head walks me round the school on arrival and explains that issues of unemployment, violence, drink, and drug abuse all have an impact on the lives of the children at the school. She should know: she has been the head here for 16 years.

A ghost needs to be laid at this point. Throughout my day at the school, during which I saw a number of lessons and spoke to a range of individuals connected with the school, nobody, at any point, even hinted at the notion that a school in such a deprived area would use its location and its circumstances as any kind of excuse for failure. This is worth mentioning because for some time it has been a favoured theme among politicians that teachers do, indeed, make such excuses. In 1999, Tony Blair believed that 'a culture of excuses still infects some part of the teaching profession' (BBC, 1999) and this was a view echoed a year later by his education secretary, David Blunkett, who told a conference of teachers that among their number there were 'cynics … who say that school performance is all about socio-economics and the areas that these schools are located in' (Carvel, 2000). A quick internet search for the link between poverty and 'excuses' for educational failure reveals a plethora of articles whose provenance is often non peer-reviewed articles from organizations in the United States. More serious research and wide-reaching research reaches more sober conclusions. Sammons and Bakkum conclude that 'education cannot remedy social exclusion by itself but remains an important means of implementing policies intended to combat social disadvantage' (Sammons and Bakkum, 2011: 9). This review of the research notes that along with the centrality of teaching and learning, backed by good leadership, it is the building of a learning community, the creation of a positive school culture, and an involvement of parents that makes a difference to children's lives and development. All of these qualities are there in abundance during my visit.

My day begins outside in the January cold with a group of five-year-olds. Every one of them seems to have a streaming and spectacularly productive cold (as do I) but they pursue their various activities of stacking planks, riding bikes (in rather orderly queues) and playing with the monster models with great energy. I am eventually requisitioned to guard the play-house, hold some bricks for a minute and give opinions on drawings as they chatter and discover in the morning frost. I am not unhappy to go into the warm where I watch Year 4 continue their number work and Year 6 do an old-fashioned piece of reading comprehension from a Roald Dahl story. I repeat a central theme of the book: there is nothing remarkable here, just good, solid lessons taking place under the guidance of well-prepared, committed teachers. Once again, classes are not arranged according to perceived ability. A good deal of individual support is available and a number of obvious adjustments made for children with particular needs. No fuss is made about any of this; it is part and parcel of how the school operates. The children – some in a basic uniform and some not (the school believes that it can have the best of both worlds and has no wish to put pressure on parents in this regard) – are cheerful and co-operative and, above all, ready to learn. Lest the reader think I am downplaying matters, there should be no equivocation here: despite the air of normalcy, this school is special.

When I talk to various adults during the course of the day this becomes even more apparent. A teacher in her second year of teaching tells me that colleagues from elsewhere and former students from her training course often ask her how she manages to teach here. She turns the question on its head by telling them that she couldn't now work anywhere else. 'You've got to have it in you to work here,' she tells me, going on to say, 'I don't want any other job. I love this job.' In her various placements as a student she became all too aware of the paperwork and the ubiquitous 'box-ticking' that bedevils the lives of teachers, and while she concedes that there is a still a degree of such practice in this school, it is kept to a minimum and the emphasis from the school's leaders is on learning in the classroom above all else. When I ask her where she thinks the difference in this school stems from she is entirely clear: from the 'passion' of the head and her deputy who have created a situation in which the school provides 'five-star nurture and support' for its pupils. In terms of assessment, the school's raw test scores place it, unsurprisingly, slightly below the national average. The teacher tells me that while they all have regard to their importance of test results, what they try to do is to 'put all our time and effort into all aspects of the children's development'. Unprompted, she invokes the term used by everyone else I interview during the course of the day when she tells me that the school is a 'family'.

It is clearly a family that does its best to welcome new members. The teacher tells me of the work that goes into integrating a new boy who, initially, was unable to join in with any collective activity of any sort. She goes on to explain how, to the great delight of all parties, the school was able to show a video clip to the boy's mother of him running in the playground and interacting with other children. The mother cries when she sees it. In a later conversation with a specialist teacher from the behaviour team working for the local authority, she tells me that of all the 23 schools in her remit, this is her 'go to' establishment when all others refuse the most difficult of children. The school takes children permanently excluded from elsewhere and its success rate in retaining them is exceptional. This specialist teacher identifies the head, the senior team, and the governors as the driving force behind this and also praises the teachers who buy into the 'values and principles' that inform the running of the school. When I press her on what she believes these values and principles to be she is entirely clear that 'it is about openness and honesty'. The school, she tells me, 'is not fearful or nervous about what it does – and that's not the case everywhere else'. She talks of the notion of family and of how the child is at the centre of what the school does at all times.

If I needed further convincing of the child-centred nature of the school, I am able to speak with a parent of five children, some of whom have been at educated primary level elsewhere, but whose younger children now attend this school, with one having moved from another establishment that, in her opinion, was 'too prim and proper'. I ask her what she means by this. She explains that her experience at other schools was the perception that both parent and child had to fit the expectation of the school itself. 'They wanted perfect children in a perfect school. They always seemed to be judging everyone.' The difference in this 'family' she tells me, is that it's not about 'numbers and statistics' but about the 'heart' of the school. This is not, she insists, just about a warm feeling of wellbeing. She talks of children being 'happy and content' and of how this 'makes a massive difference to learning'. She wants to know how her children are getting on, but not through constant testing and assessment. 'I'm all for intelligent children,' she tells me, 'but testing isn't always going to tell you how much a child is learning.' She talks of trusting teachers, as she does, to ensure that learning is taking place.

In a further example of the school's complete commitment to inclusivity, I am introduced to the person who has established and runs the forest school. It is worth making an immediate point here: there is no forest either in the school grounds, in the immediate vicinity or for some few miles around it. In fact, as the forest school teacher tells me rather gleefully, there isn't even a single tree anywhere near. The philosophy behind forest schools (see forestschoolsasssociation.org) is about establishing an outdoor space where children learn to act independently and develop positive attitudes to learning as they explore and experience the natural world for themselves. The forest school here is a requisitioned corner of the playground next to the modest playing field that abuts the school. An old Belfast sink dug into the ground serves as a pond, various wooden structures for sitting and play are ranged around a central fire – where real fires are built and maintained – and all tools and implements are the real thing. Plastic is not allowed. On the days when the forest school teacher is present activities take place irrespective of any adverse weather. At present the forest school only runs on certain days and can only accommodate a very few pupils: others, I am told, look on enviously. When I ask what the value of the enterprise is perceived as being the teacher is clear; not everyone, she tells me, learns by sitting down and writing. In the forest school children feel free from scrutiny and judgement. 'They feel special,' she tells me. 'We don't just pack them in and tell them what to do.' She expresses frustration that some of the skills and socialization learnt here are not acknowledged as part of a child's progress and development. Above all, she is annoyed that accountability, which she accepts as an article of faith, all boils down to measurable test results rather than these broader accomplishments.

Four themes run through the commentary and observations of these adults. The first of these is the idea that the school is a family, where, as a couple of comments acknowledge, there is occasional falling out but that, for the vast majority of time, pulls together and cares for everyone. Second, there is a great sense of trust. This exists between all staff – teaching and non-teaching alike – and the school's leaders. It is there between the school and its parents as well as with outside agencies. It exists between teachers and pupils, working to the benefit of all parties. Third, there is a theme common to dozens of remarks from primary teachers that I have heard when conducting this research: they are burdened by a curriculum that is too crowded, too superficial and over-complicated. As an example, I often find myself in conversation with primary teachers, as I do at this school, about the knowledge of linguistic terminology required of ten-year-olds that, as the holder of a master's degree in literature, I find both baffling and unhelpful. As the parent to whom I spoke points out, it's all very well asking parents to help with children's work, but when the demands of the curriculum change so frequently, this is easier said than done.

The final common point relates to a question I put to all respondents from this school: if you had the chance, what would you say to the government minister in charge of education? The response is almost unanimous: she (Justine Greening was in post at the time of the visit) should come here for a day to see what goes on. A teacher tells me that 'some children haven't been smiled at before they get here in the morning and plenty haven't had breakfast'. The forest school teacher is furious that the school can be held accountable for punctuality and attendance in circumstances where there are some children who, through no fault of their own, live chaotic lives. There are things, says the specialist teacher, that you just can't measure 'and this school provides them. Some things aren't quantifiable.' The forest school teacher suspects that ministers 'must just look at leafy glade schools without realizing that we have to the best that we can with our children here'. Even given that these respondents are all from the local area and probably have historic reasons for mistrusting central government, these comments indicate that while the school itself runs on trust, that quality is demonstrably missing in the relationship with their political masters.

To restate the point; nobody is looking for excuses. What I see in the school is excellent practice from accomplished teachers committed to giving the pupils the best chances they can. But they are not operating on equal terms with schools and pupils elsewhere. As if to illustrate this, a topical example falls into my lap as I move towards finishing the draft of this chapter.

The news story comes from the secondary sector, but it is a telling one all the same. In February 2017 it was revealed that students in the independent, private sector took greater advantage of the provision to use extra time in examinations than those in the state sector (Bateman, 2017). In an almost charmingly disingenuous comment, a headteacher from the private sector explains that such schools are more able to apply for help 'because of ever-improving monitoring and awareness of special needs' as well as being 'fortunate to have proper resourcing and specialist departments, which can be lacking in state maintained schools'. In case it needs spelling out we have a situation in which schools that already start from an advantageous position in terms of funding, staffing and overall resourcing are better placed to take advantage of measures put in place to help those who start from a less privileged position. Any reader or observer would be excused for resorting to clichés about the rich getting richer while the poor get poorer. In the context of a school battling to make provision for disadvantaged children in a disadvantaged area, this news item must seem like something of a sick metaphor for a system that has scant regard for its need and that of the community it serves.

Chapter 9

Learning in your slippers

What might home-schooling tell us about schools and
pedagogy?

Paulo Freire's seminal text *The Pedagogy of the Oppressed,* originally
published in 1968, rarely seems to make its way onto the crowded
programme for those training to become teachers. This is regrettable:
much of what he wrote half a century ago has great resonance. Freire was
concerned that education was being reduced to a 'depositing' exercise, based
on the idea of suitable knowledge being something outside the experience
of the learner – an alien concept to be mastered and controlled with the
help of a teacher. In such circumstances the school curriculum becomes
something to be reified, organized, and consumed. He captures this thought
in this passage when he talks of how teaching and learning 'becomes an
act of depositing, in which students are the depositories and the teacher is
the depositor. Instead of communication, the teacher issues communiqués
and "makes deposits" which the students patiently receive, memorize and
repeat' (Freire, 1990: 45).

A few years after the publication of Freire's work, Ivan Illich wrote
Deschooling Society in which he talked of how 'most learning is not the
result of instruction. It is rather the result of unhampered participation
in a meaningful setting. Most people learn best by being "with it," yet
school makes them identify their personal, cognitive growth with elaborate
planning and manipulation' (Illich, 1976: 39). With these challenges to the
school system in mind, I took a chance by exploring an alternative sort of
provision. The chapter that follows looks at home-schooling. It is by no
means uncritical advocacy – but it may give us pause for thought and there's
some cheery stuff here as well. I'll begin by providing some context.

Until very recently, an enjoyable part of my professional duties was
teaching on an education foundation degree, leading a module entitled
Contemporary Issues in Education. Most students were female and from
what the higher education sector identifies as a 'widening participation'
background. My job was to seek out educational issues of the day and
investigate them with this group, looking at how they were treated by the
media, on social networks and, ultimately, by academic opinion. The great
flexibility offered by this brief made this one of my favourite parts of the

academic year and, in this age of perpetual quest for client satisfaction, was highly rated by the students themselves. When, by complete chance, I came across Christine, a local home-educator, I thought this was too good an opportunity to miss and asked her if she was willing to come to talk to the group, which she duly did. I told her to be prepared here for some robust questioning and was reassured by her response that she doubted that she would be hearing anything that she hadn't previously been challenged with.

Christine comes to the session armed with a PowerPoint presentation that she informs us has been put together with the help of the middle of her five children, and in which she is a little inexpert: it is only fair to point out that by the time of subsequent visits, she has completely mastered the technology. She shows us something of what her children – along with other home-educated children in her area – experience and gives us a flavour of the different approach to learning that comes with this. Her audience listens politely and then the questions start. I would wager that these are a reflection of those asked by any group of people about this issue.

Aren't these children lacking in social skills? How can they possibly relate to peers? In what ways is this preparation for the 'real world' outside their cosy circumstances? Where is the line drawn between parent and teacher? They are surprised – as am I – that there is no structured working day; like them, I expected a degree of regimentation replicating normal school hours. They are outraged – as am I, if I'm truthful – that lazing in bed is an option if a child decides that there is nothing that can be fruitfully done by getting up. They are envious, however, of the fact that a project once started – reading a book, doing some sewing, making a model – can be pursued without interruption. They pose tricky questions: in particular, how are children safeguarded against abuse and, perhaps most astutely, isn't this just something rich people can do? After all, five children, one income and a large house – these are hardly common conditions for most people.

Christine responds by showing an array of pictures of children associating with their peers at organizations like Scouts and Guides. We see them playing football at the local leisure centre and there are pictures of children listening to elderly neighbours or working with visiting, native speakers to learn languages together. We are entertained by stories and pictures of a self-produced play, staged in the garden in summer for their own delight. Voluntary and charity actions are woven into their routines. Apart from the fact that I see them as indisputably privileged, there is nothing odd, peculiar or over-nerdy about what is going on.

What becomes clear from the question and answer session is that the decision as to whether or not they wish to attend school is one that has been left to the children themselves. The original choice, taken some 20 years since, arose when her eldest child, described by Christine as inquisitive and articulate, became increasingly sad and frustrated by not having time to draw pictures at school. Thinking this a temporary blip, Christine tells him to soldier on, but as he does so it is not just the lack of this opportunity that upsets him, but a general lack of both creativity and, as he sees it, energy from other children whom he precociously characterizes as sloths (we go often to the Natural History Museum) that contribute to his unhappiness. A visit to the school, which she undertakes with some reluctance over being thought cranky or pushy, fails to reassure Christine. When enquiring about any more space for her child's artistic interests, she is told that in an ever more crowded curriculum art in particular tends to get squeezed out.

After a good deal of soul-searching, along with some opposition and opprobrium from family and acquaintances, she made the decision to home-educate with a view to his gradually going to school. She tells us that she didn't even know that she was interested in home-education, that she certainly did not regard herself as a rebel and that, in all honesty, she thought that her child would decide to go to school sooner rather than later. She wanted, above all, to be a good parent, but what she saw when her child was in school was the transformation from a busy and active boy to one who began to doubt his abilities and who was being deprived of the things that, in her view, would make him into a well-rounded, educated person.

The undergraduate students listen with great interest ... but with enduring scepticism. At the end of the session a number of them crowd round her to ask the questions they lacked the confidence to pose in open forum – a good sign that a session has been a success. When I conduct some rudimentary market-research of my own about the inclusion of this topic on the module, I am told unequivocally to keep it in for future years – which has happened with similar success and response. There is no doubting the respect that Christine and her actions have earned from these young people, albeit that many, in the kindest of ways, consider her slightly barmy.

The government's education website is terse and minimal in its commentary about the choice to home-school, confirming that it is legal and that some help may be available from local councils. Parents or carers are advised that checks may be carried out on them if they make this decision; otherwise, it is fair to say the information provided is factual and non-committal. The extent of home-schooling in England is uncertain, but at the time of writing, it does seem to be on the rise (Lees, 2014). Responses to Freedom of Information Requests from local authorities at the end of 2015 (Jeffreys, 2015) indicated a 65 per cent increase over six years in the number of children being home-educated, although this needs to put into the context of one child out of every 250 of school age being educated in this way. From the information gathered, the reasons for choosing home education mirrors that of significant research projects in recent years (Kraftl, 2013; Lees, 2014) and are unsurprising. The principal motive given is a difference of philosophy and lifestyle and this is followed by being in dispute with local authorities over the allocation of school places. At the time of writing this particular reason is much more prevalent in those areas where there are selective grammar schools. Although information about faith and religion was not gathered in all cases, 31 per cent of home-educators identify this as an important reason for their choice and, of these, half identify as Christian and one-third as Muslim. The scepticism of myself and my own students about this being a middle-class preserve is partially borne out by the data. The best estimates indicate that in the UK 15 per cent of home-educators are working class, although while 76 per cent of US home-educators held college degrees or above, this only applied to 49 per cent of instances in the UK (Kraftl, 2013).

All of the research, or even a quick google trawl about home-schooling, identifies one rather startling piece of information, which is that the label 'home-schooling' is something of a misnomer. Like my own students, I imagined replication of a routine school day with breakfast being cleared from the table before embarking on a regimen of subject-related activities, with the day being punctuated by the usual rhythms of break and play as appropriate. One of the principal characteristics of home-schooling is that much of it takes place beyond the home; parks, museums, libraries, and local spaces become central to what happens in a 'normal' day. Flexibility and spontaneity underpin much that takes place along with an encouragement of self-reliance and independence among the children themselves. All of which reminds me to reiterate that this chapter is not advocacy for an approach that may be beyond the scope, ambition or plain old expense of most people, but a glimpse into the ideal of what education could be if it did not operate within a system that demands it be treated as a commodity to be packaged, delivered, measured and ascribed market value.

I contact Christine to ask if I can observe her and her children in action as part of the research for this book. She reminds me that the two eldest are now at university and that the middle child goes to sixth-form for some lessons, but that I am welcome to visit. During our conversation we return to some of the issues we had touched upon when she spoke to my students. Talking of the traditional academic success of her two eldest sons she is adamant that 'they have achieved because they have had so much freedom' and of how surprised the boys themselves were at the boredom they perceived among their peers when they went to school in their later teens. She talks of how 'I never thought I knew best' and, once again, of her constant striving to be the 'good parent'. We laugh at an anecdote about how, at a social gathering, an adult expresses delight that 'your children are playing with the others'. She reminds me that she had briefly been a secondary teacher and had decided that it wasn't for her, but that she had been hugely influenced by the writing of John Holt.

I suspect that the works of John Holt are now almost unknown by those training to enter the profession. I am entertained that an internet search brings the late and eminent reggae singer as the first entry with Holt the educator pushed down the page. I am at pains to point out that in the critique I offer of the current system of education, none of it is underpinned by the notion of a golden age. So while it is true that as a student teacher I was intrigued and influenced by Holt's two seminal works from the mid-1960s – *How Children Learn* and *How Children Fail* – I am quite certain that his thoughts and ideas went unnoticed by many of my contemporaries. Nonetheless, these were core texts given to us as provocations and stimuli. Much of what Holt has to say – and I do not buy wholesale his vision for education, including his advocacy for home-schooling – is contentious and I consider some of his conclusions based on impression rather than rigorous research. For all that, notions of alternative education were presented to us in order for us to hone and justify our own position as beginning, institution-based, traditional teachers. We were introduced to ideas about pedagogy, knowledge and socialization that challenged what we thought we knew. This 'theoretical' stuff, so despised by senior politicians, encouraged us to tackle the basic question of what education is for – a challenge that, quite properly still engages thoughtful teachers.

During their period of training, most teachers develop a reasonable acquaintance with the principal thinkers about pedagogy and learning such as Piaget, Bruner, Vygotsky and, at the very least, become familiar with the notion that children learn in different and uneven ways. Their earliest encounters with children in formal settings provide them with ample, immediate evidence of this and thus they are able to make connections between theory and real life. However, at this point a model of education that requires proof of outcome and measurable results is superimposed on children as they go about this messy business of trying to make sense of the world, constructing their knowledge with the help of adults and 'knowledgeable others'. Teachers now find themselves in a system where children and those outside the family responsible for their care and development have to demonstrate – and find proof of achievement of – a whole range of skills and abilities. The question that often goes unasked, however, is 'for what purpose?' Although the needs of whichever assessment system is currently in vogue may be met, the purpose of all of this measuring and definition by numbers and criteria remains unclear.

A glance at the statutory framework for early years foundation stage (EYFS) (DfE, 2014) is revealing. The document talks of the requirement to instil literacy and numeracy skills for children below five years of age as well as developing an understanding of the world and of encouraging creativity. Leaving aside the fact that those countries that regularly perform better than the UK in international league tables for educational achievement often don't want children in any formal setting until they're much older than five (OECD, 2016) this is unremarkable enough. It is not unreasonable to want children to be able to develop these important skills at an early age if they are comfortable doing so. The key to the purpose of the EYFS, however, is revealed in a sentence in the introduction to the document: the framework, we are told, is in place to promote 'teaching and learning to ensure children's "school readiness"' (DfE, 2014: 5 – original inverted commas). In the section that deals with the assessment of these children, we are informed that Year 1 teachers must be given a copy of the Profile report together with a short commentary on each child's skills and abilities' (DfE, 2014: 14). It does not, of course, make reference to the fact that the inspectoral body, the Office for Standards in Education (Ofsted), will also be looking at these outcomes in order to assess the viability of a particular setting. What we are doing is setting young people off on the road to a constant assessment of their 'readiness' to proceed to the next stage … and this is just the beginning of the process.

This notion of 'readiness' becomes embedded in the consciousness and actions of schools and teachers whose production of results has become the *sine qua non* of what they are forced to do. In *Teachers Undefeated* (p.26) I tell the story of a school that drives as many children through examinations as quickly as possible for the dual purpose of boosting overall results and then moving those same children on to yet more examinations and the acquisition of yet more results – all at the expense of any possibility of genuine learning taking place. When Vygotsky famously talks of the Zone of Proximal Development, this is not quite what he had in mind. Yet this notion of 'preparation' is ubiquitous in the English system: EYFS makes children 'school ready'; Key Stage 2 assessments at 11 are preparation for the 'real thing' when secondary school comes along; the justification for the discredited (but still often informally conducted) Key Stage 3 assessment at

14 was that it, in its turn, was preparation for 'proper exams' … and so the tale continues.

In a touching, yet slightly dispiriting, episode during my researches, this idea of being ever-ready for the next step is expounded for me by an engaging ten-year-old child. Talking to me about school with a group of his peers, the subject of Key Stage 2 SATs arises. He's not nervous about them, he assures me, and his confident manner would suggest that he is being completely truthful. After all, he tells me, if he does well in these tests – and he expects to do so – he'll be put in the 'clever classes' at secondary and because of this he'll do well in his GCSEs because he'll have had practice at tests and then he'll do A levels and then he'll go to university and, as a consequence, get a good job. I hope with all my heart that he does, but I also hope that at some point he manages to get off the preparation treadmill that he has been on since the state first took an interest in his education. He seems a happy, well-adjusted child and he tells me that he loves his primary school. Nonetheless, his view of the education system and how to navigate through it successfully is a long way from what Christine and, it appears her children, want for themselves.

I visit Christine's home on bright autumnal morning. It is 10 o'clock and the rest of the world is already going about its business as I arrive. Her two younger daughters, Anthea (11) and Beth (14) are at home this morning and I am warned that the former is having a 'bit of a moment'. Whether out of deference to my presence or as result of having some late breakfast, this moment passes with no incident whatsoever. The three older children – all boys – are not present. Two are at various stages of their university education and the youngest of them has chosen to go to the sixth form of his local comprehensive – a choice made by all of the boys in their later teens. The large house is cheerfully chaotic: books and ipads litter the table in the main room, jostling for space with newspapers, novels, standard workbooks and deserted bits of breakfast. A handful of cats come and go as they please, occasionally finding themselves the object of affectionate grabbing from Anthea who tells me, somewhat implausibly as she buries her face in their fur, that she is allergic to them. Meanwhile, Beth sits contentedly at the end of the table working her way through mathematical equations, contributing to the general chatter in a desultory way before returning to the task in hand.

Cardboard boxes are piled around and these are the result of clothes collections for Syrian refugees with which the whole household has been involved. A day – a school day, if that is how we may choose in these circumstances to describe it – has already been spent in sorting and organizing these donations, along with some conversation about the situation that has prompted the need for such collections. We consider a number of ideas: the way in which people's charitable instincts (they have been overwhelmed by the volume of donations) come to the fore and how, in some ways, it is also an expression of helplessness – the only thing they can do. Beth tells the heart-breaking tale of how a small child's cardigan had been donated from a parent who had lost that child and decided that this was a proper use to which to put it. At Christine's prompting, Anthea tells me that even though they are collecting for winter clothes, she insisted that they include a flimsy party dress because, no matter how grim the circumstances, it might be just the thing to cheer up a little girl. From time to time Beth returns to her equations. After a continued conversation during which I clumsily try to explain how the fall of Ceausescu in Romania led to the proliferation of uncared-for orphans – we had strayed into talking about local charity shops – and about the successful operation on one of the cats, Anthea shows me her pet turtles and decides that she's going to make biscuits this morning.

As we look at the two creatures sliding uncertainly about on the now cat-free table, we speculate about which senses they rely on most. Christine consults her iphone and tells us, to our great delight, that they have three ears, the extra one being on the end of the nose. Some careful but slimy investigation fails to confirm this as the apertures are, apparently, tiny. One beast who revels, with some justification, in the name of Speedy, causes a few moments of alarm as he makes his way across the table and so we decide it is time to return the turtles to the water, Beth to her equations and Anthea to her biscuit making. I ask Beth how she manages the intricacies of the maths and she tells me that a combination of online videos and co-operation with her mum means that she finds her way along just fine and that it's a subject she really enjoys … and when she get stuck, her dad is the one who can help her out if need be. She reels off the list of very traditional GCSEs she hopes to enter in due course: she has not yet chosen to go to school and, indeed, may not do so. In the kitchen Anthea consults her mother's ipad for the biscuit recipe and goes about collecting the ingredients. Christine's role in all of these proceedings is advisory with the occasional meaningful prompt: the girls' default position appears to be that of most children when learning, which is to apply degrees of either selective deafness or attention as they deem appropriate.

The biscuit-making develops into something of a co-operative exercise. Anthea collects most of the ingredients, begins to measure items out and starts mixing. Beth decides that equations can wait for a few moments while she lends a hand. The measurement of 85 grams of treacle using some antiquated scales and an incomplete set of weights would make a brilliant exemplar lesson in mathematical reasoning. We stray into conversation about the use of mobile phones – there are some firm family rules about the limitation of their use, albeit that all of the children have their own – and both girls demonstrate a clear understanding and appreciation of current debates about the damaging effects on friendships, wellbeing and self-esteem that are exercising society. And then Beth produces her own phone to show some stylish, funny and to my untutored eye really rather well-made music videos that she has produced with a group of friends. At this point, Beth disappears upstairs to 'learn some spellings' and Christine commandeers the last stages of mixing the biscuit dough.

Christine and I chatter as we wait for the biscuits to bake and review some of our earlier conversations about learning and the ways and speeds at which children develop. Her oldest son is on the verge of completing a structural engineering degree having discovered his own liking for maths after completing his GCSE at grade B and then going to school – for the first time – to complete an A level for which he gained an A-star grade. I am reminded of an earlier conversation with Christine in which she explains how, as a little boy, he had become obsessed with spaces – what would be damaged if that tree fell down, how could that table ever fit into that corner – before addressing any formal maths. I trade stories about young people I have known and taught over the years who, in popular teacher vernacular, just didn't get it – or want to get it – until they were good and ready. The biscuits emerge and, although variegated in shape and size, are delicious and a morning has passed.

I repeat that none of this is an unalloyed advocacy of home-schooling and my reservations remain firmly in place. Readers, like my undergraduate class, are more than entitled to maintain their belief that, for it all, this is not preparation for the real world and that just because some rather privileged children, aided and abetted by parents and a local community with the resources to support them, can achieve traditional examination success, this proves nothing. Much the same argument is often applied to a range of what might be dubbed 'alternative' approaches to education as epitomized in settings such as Montessori schools, the Reggio Emilia approach and, most famously, Summerhill School. There is a convincing point of view that states this sort of indulgence might be all well and good for those with the money and confidence to allow children to find their feet eventually, but for most of us, this leisurely approach to education is a chance we're not prepared to take.

It is interesting here to look at the private sector, which educates around eight per cent of children in the UK (ISC, 2017). Although examination results are consistently good, such schools remain relaxed about their importance. The website of the ISC rather primly announces that 'although ISC does not produce or endorse "school league tables" this information is used by the press to produce their independent school tables' (ISC, 2016). A trawl through the websites of such schools reveals an emphasis on producing well-rounded individuals capable of engaging in a range of pursuits and activities that go beyond examination success. In a well-documented example, this small percentage of privately educated people won one-third of the medals at the last two Olympic Games (Sutton Trust, 2016), revealing the differing emphases afforded (literally) to such activities by different sectors. Beyond this, however, there is no escaping the fact that the scale of exam success is advertised as an important and influential factor, and almost, it could be argued, as an obvious fact.

Arguments about such freedom and latitude being the preserve of those who enjoy privilege and advantage make perfect sense. I would contend, however, that they do not negate the wider argument about the need to discover what a child knows, understands and can do, and to allow that child to work, within some limits, towards achieving this without the constant burden of checking its progress. What is more, that child does not need its development relentlessly compared with peers who, in their turn, may be developing different skills and abilities at different rates. The comments of a Grace teacher from *Teachers Undefeated* (p.63) fit perfectly here as he entertains his teaching colleagues with the observation that they are encouraged to differentiate for their children in a thousand different ways before getting them all to sit the same test at the same time. During the national campaigns against the SATs two handy epigrams were often invoked: a pig doesn't get any fatter through constant weighing and the best way of checking a plant's growth is not to keep digging it up. These alternative settings, along with the private sector, deliberately eschew such practices, confident in the knowledge that there is no need to engage with them. I do not mean to be insulting in any way when I say that such an approach may not always be informed by any deep knowledge of learning and pedagogy on the part of those who run such settings. I suspect that more often than not their actions are informed more by established practice and precedent. Neither do I suggest that such settings are bastions of liberalism and open-mindedness when it comes to notions of educating the whole child. What is clear, however, is that room is made to follow pursuits and ideas that contribute to a wider education than one solely dictated to by test results and outcomes.

The value of this wider education is universally recognized and although there is no evidence of a causal relationship between engagement with issues beyond the classroom and academic success, there remains an observable link between young people who take part in a range of different activities and their achievements in school (Shulruf, 2010). The idea that the quest for this 'well-roundedness' is becoming more difficult is captured in the *Warwick Commission on the Future of Cultural Values in the UK* (University of Warwick, 2015). The report points to an alarming drop – as high as 50 per cent in some areas – in the number of young people studying design- and arts-based subjects; it identifies the fact that just over eight per cent of students at 16 years of age choose to study a combination of arts and science subjects and, in terms of wider access to experience beyond the classroom, it reveals that there is now something of a two-tier system with a distinct danger that opportunities for wider involvement could be 'limited to the socially advantaged and the privately educated' (p.44). When it comes to creativity and enterprise, qualities one would imagine that might be important to international capitalism and its supporters, the report draws the conclusion that 'the English education system does not provide or encourage either of these priorities and this will negatively impact not just on the future of the creative industries but on our capacity to produce creative, world-leading scientists, engineers and technologists' (p.15).

Despite all of the valid reservations that endure about home-schooling, it would appear that Christine is right to be worried about the lack of space for creativity, experimentation or just plain old wondering that is afforded to children in school. The home-schooling community is attempting to foster a model of personal growth for children at every turn. It may not be an option open to all, but for this small community the test is very much in its place.

Chapter 10

So, what are we going to do about it?

How to put the test in its place

I sit in the staff room during one of my research visits and I chat away to someone who is something of a rarity – a middle-aged male primary school teacher. He asks me about my work and we drift into general conversation about many of the ideas that have dominated this book. Principal among these is the notion that there is too much that gets in the way of the straightforward business of learning and teaching. Like so many of the teachers to whom I have spoken in the past few years, he tells me that he tries to fight against becoming disheartened and frequently reminds himself of why this is his chosen profession. In a jocular, good-natured way just before we part, he asks me, 'well, what are you going to do about it all?' It's a good question, but I do have a ready answer. I tell him that I'm going to write about it, acknowledging that this first part of the response sounds lame. I go on to explain that I do so in the hope that teachers who read what I write take comfort – and strength – from knowing that there are plenty of like-minded people out there who share their values and attitudes. He nods approvingly: it's a reasonable premise. However, as gratifying as this approbation is, writing about the situation can only be the start. For teachers, parents and academics to make a genuine impact on the hegemony of testing and the infection of the GERM, collective action is necessary. This chapter draws together the main conclusions from the research behind this book before looking at ways in which such action can be implemented.

What is to be learnt from the eight settings whose experiences form the central part of this book? Any attempt to catalogue such findings into an over-simplified list risks not doing justice to the multi-faceted approach of the heads, teachers and others involved. There are, however, clear and obvious points of correspondence in all of these places. The first and most important is the establishing of a school that has values and attitudes that are fully shared and feed seamlessly into daily practice. To reiterate a point made elsewhere, this goes beyond laminated aphorisms, banners on railings, and noble statements on websites and in handbooks. It is about ensuring that a culture and set of behaviours are seen by all as a code by which life is lived in that institution. This may sound a touch evangelical, even cult-like; it is no such thing. It manifests itself by ensuring that the genuine needs of all children are placed at the centre of what takes place. This requires open, honest discussion between teachers at all levels as well as those who work to support them. Trust is central to this approach and in particular trust that teachers will do the right thing and the understanding that this may well result in the occasional mistake or error of judgement.

The second feature that distinguishes these schools is a belief in mixed-ability teaching. Chapter 5 dealt with the deep-seated, almost evangelical, opposition to this notion in some detail. The fundamental problem with this opposition is that it buys into the concept that intelligence is fixed and has limits to how far and in what directions it can develop. It subscribes to an idea that there are chronological way-markers that people that should reach at pre-determined points in their lives and, above all, within the school system it means that even if a child runs hard to catch a particular bus, once it's been missed, there won't be another coming along any time soon. The schools in this study adopt a more thoughtful and intelligent approach to how human beings develop. They know that this development is uneven, often unpredictable, and that by setting and streaming children, particularly within a curriculum that becomes ever more narrow, the chances for missing potential and ability are acute.

The third common aspect is that of encouraging teachers to behave autonomously. Chapter 2 exposed the notion of false or 'earned' autonomy stemming from a set of circumstances where such autonomy needs to be circumscribed by a narrow set of actions leading to pre-set outcomes. The schools in this book do not see it in this way. There is an understanding that responsibilities will not be shirked and that every effort will be made to ensure that children learn and, when necessary, perform to the best of their ability in tests. Sometimes this results in individual lessons that go off-track or even – that greatest of iniquities in modern schooling – one where writing does not take place. These are not cataclysmic events: they are, at worst, simple errors that can be rectified, reflected on, and avoided in the future. There is proper, professional scrutiny of what happens but in most cases this is collegiate rather than overtly managerial.

There is a confidence in these schools that they are doing the right thing by pupils and parents. It is important to understand that this does not come solely from heroic heads and managers, but their taking the lead in such matters is the only way in which open dialogue and honesty about teaching and learning can take place. Actions are informed by an understanding of how children learn and how, in turn, pedagogic approaches need to be adapted to circumstance. In many cases these schools are committed to active professional development that allows teachers to pursue knowledge and understanding in these important areas – going beyond day-courses looking for instant solutions and quick results. There is an appreciation that subject knowledge, be this subject-specific or more general in terms of pedagogy, is axiomatic to engaging children and leads to learning that is deep and sustainable. It is notable that in these schools staff turnover is low. There is a culture of keeping working hours under control and of taking proper breaks during the day. The literal and metaphorical spaces for staff to discuss ideas have not been closed down. This confidence becomes an institutional, not a personal, characteristic. From it, and from the models of learning and teaching that are enabled to develop, we can begin to look at how such settings could become the norm and not the exception.

In a series of interviews with commentators and campaigners I discuss what I have found in this book and in *Teachers Undefeated* and ask how they believe the important issue of putting the test in its place can be promoted. The line of argument that emerges from these interviews is clear. First, all interested parties need to be as fully informed and as knowledgeable about Sahlberg's GERM and its effects as possible. Second, they need to use this knowledge to act collectively in order to oppose it. I begin by talking to one of the most knowledgeable people around.

I meet investigative journalist Warwick Mansell whom I first met some ten years ago prior to the publication of his illuminating and authoritative book, *Education by Numbers* (Mansell, 2007). Mansell's forensic analysis and research demonstrated that teaching to the test produced a whole range of unwanted consequences, from 'gaming' by schools in order to get the best published outcomes, to detrimental effects in terms of producing a well-rounded education and a broad curriculum. Above all the emphasis on testing did not produce the raising of standards that was meant to justify their importance. He has spent the succeeding decade exposing much of the hypocrisy, dishonesty and concealment of information that has been behind the drive to privatize and standardize education in England. Given the esteem in which he is held by so many in the world of education I am astonished to hear from him that his highly respected column in a national newspaper is to be discontinued. Meeting as we do at a time when 'fake news' is a major item in international media, we can only express our bemusement at this.

I begin by asking him how he thinks educational matters, specifically as they pertain to testing, have developed in the last decade. He is unequivocal in his response: things have got worse. He jokes that he seems to have been writing the same story for the last ten years. He talks of how the pressure on schools to get results seems to be at the bottom of many of his investigative stories. He is appalled at the extent to which schools manipulate numbers on roll to improve percentage pass rates and is concerned by the outcome of his investigations that reveal the extent to which 'troublesome' pupils are removed from school, either temporarily or permanently, because of this. I am astonished when he tells me that his inquiries have shown that one in four headteachers has experience of this.

Guy Robert-Holmes and Alice Bradbury (see Chapter 4) identify the troubling notion of the 'datafication' of the child and Mansell shares their discomfort. It is an idea to which we will return later in this chapter. In particular he talks of how his work traces the deleterious effects of a system where 'everything becomes about the reputation of the institution'. He argues that what this has led to is a situation where logic is turned on its head. Successive governments make pledges to improve the standard of education in our schools; inevitably, problems occur when targets – often arbitrarily imposed – are not met or even exceeded. The response to such problems has not been to look at the curriculum, pedagogy, age-appropriateness or societal relevance of what is on offer, but to simply say, 'there is a problem here, so the way to deal with it is to reform the indicators'. The datafication process then becomes complete: what matters is not a child who knows and understands something, but finding a way to capture that child as a single integer to be collated and judged. Mansell, much of whose recent work has been exposing scandalous behaviour in academy chains (*The Guardian*, n.d.), sees a clear link between this overt commercialization of education and the treatment of children as mere statistics.

Mansell's work contributes to that of a burgeoning network of commentators and activists who challenge the current model of testing and commercialization. The organization *More Than a Score* (morethanascore. co.uk) is a coalition of 18 organizations including experts in children's literacy, childhood welfare, psychotherapists, educational researchers, bodies opposed to testing, and those dedicated to upholding a rich and varied approach to education and child development. I visit one of its principal members, journalist and film-maker Madeleine Holt.

Holt tells me of the root of her interest. Her father, Maurice, was the founder of the slow education movement. His explanation of the principles behind this movement stands as a clear rebuttal of what occurs in many schools and as a credo for what brings this coalition of organizations together:

The notion of slow is essentially about establishing a *process* that fosters intensity and understanding and equips students to reason for themselves. An essential aim is fostering the ability to understand in depth, and the arts of *deliberation* are an essential element in this. In slow education, the concept of *process* is central to the way the curriculum is conceived and experienced: what is abhorrent is the notion of *delivery,* and this distinguishes the slow curriculum from one driven by *outcomes.*

(Holt, 2014)

Beyond this familial connection she is a parent with children at various stages in the school system and has dedicated a good deal of time and thought, personally and professionally, to 'what makes a child prosper and the comprehensive ideal'. She is entirely clear about what she perceives to be the purpose of *More Than a Score.* She talks of a 'sense of uneasiness among parents' and of them being 'emotionally uneasy' about the current testing regime, seeing this coalition as a way of working with parents to 'decipher the educational landscape which is increasingly opaque'. She identifies the source of this disquiet residing in the fact that children are being 'drilled' when they are not developmentally ready for such a high-stakes exercise. She hopes for more parental boycotts of SATs test and of these 18 organizations developing into a parental movement that will mount a continuing challenge as a 'network of parents and professionals working at grass-roots'. She is insistent that the work of these organizations is not party-political, but concedes that their activities are, by default, political. It is, she tells me, about galvanizing the work of all of them so that their oppositional voices can be heard.

I press her on the term 'galvanizing'; what does this mean in terms of what actually happens? She talks to me of conferences and regional meetings attended by professionals and parents; supporting statements have been garnered from eminent figures from the public school system – to which she is opposed in principle but whose views are worth courting 'because they're more likely to be listened to'. There have been contributions to parliamentary select committees and the dissemination of their ideas through a range of websites. In an echo of my earlier comment about writing being a medium through which oppositional ideas can be broadcast, she tells me of a film she is about to make in a primary school in the north-west whose headteacher is adamant that 'tests will not drive the school'. I express some disappointment I hadn't located this head as a potential respondent, along with another to whom she referred earlier, as this may have made for an interesting contribution to my research. Holt makes the point that what we need is a directory of such schools. She is right and I express the hope that working in our different ways we may be able to locate more such institutions and set up just such a repository of information. Driving all of her actions is a determination that this coalition of various campaigning bodies can bring together a well-informed collection of interested parties prepared to take action to challenge standardization and commodification and to seek an 'alternative, coherent vision' for education.

I do not push Holt on the value of appealing to the parliamentary select committee on education, but it is worth a brief digression to look at the work of that body. These committees are cross-party and there is a traditional, albeit occasionally contested view that this is where the 'real work' of government is done. In September 2016 an inquiry into primary assessment was instigated. In the words of the Chair, Conservative MP Ian Carmichael, the inquiry was necessary because 'news of SATs boycotts in certain parts of the country and data showing almost half of pupils in England failed to meet the new tough standards in reading, writing, and maths point to unresolved issues in the way we prepare our children for secondary school and help them reach their potential' (UK Parliament, 2016). As a principal adviser to the committee, Professor Jo-Anne Baird from the University of Oxford echoed Carmichael's concern, identifying 'broad(er) questions about the suitability of the primary assessments. They have had little evaluation since their introduction. The experts who were involved in devising this national curriculum … were unable to agree on the final content' (ibid). Such reflexivity and caution is not reproduced in the contribution of schools' minister Nick Gibb to the inquiry. In his view all is for the best in the best of all possible worlds:

> I am very comfortable with the work that was produced by the expert panel and the results that came out of the consultation on that curriculum; I think it is a curriculum we can be proud of. It is a step up, a significant step up, from where we have been.
> (Nick Gibb, oral evidence to the select committee inquiry. Ibid.)

Educational campaigners have become accustomed to the fierce resistance of those in power to anything so trite as research, scholarship or expert opinion (see Chapter 4). If they needed any reminder of the need to organize on all fronts and with the help of all interested bodies, this further example of the triumph of ideology over evidence should serve that purpose.

Someone who requires no such reminder is seasoned educational campaigner Sara Tomlinson. A veteran activist on a number of fronts, currently including serving on the steering committee of *More Than a Score*, I ask her how and why she manages to keep going. Her answer is unequivocal: 'you just know you've got to do the right thing by children'. Her involvement in campaigns against SATs, baseline testing, and in the creation of the Primary Charter is political as well as pedagogical. She points to the way in which commercial assessment packages have burgeoned in the last decade – a simple internet search will reveal just how extensive this particular market is – and makes a clear connection between this and the way in which standardized testing, a principal feature of the GERM, is linked firmly to privatization. Like all campaigners she knows the value of parental support and in particular she acknowledges that there is an emotional as well as a rational aspect to garnering this support. Even given the effect it has on children in terms of unnecessary pressure at inappropriate times in their lives, she suggests that 'people don't like their children's education being sold out to the highest bidder.' She too is frustrated at the unwillingness of those in power to recognize scholarship, research and expert opinion. She is particularly outraged at the dogmatic, unproven approach in England that attempts to formalize children's education so much more quickly than in those countries, Finland in particular, who realized some time ago that a more relaxed approach yields better outcomes in the long run. She deplores the 'data shadow that follows every child around'. We finish our conversation by her talking of this shadow being part of something much wider concerning the way in which society views children as a whole. She invokes Sharon Beder's excellent volume *This Little Kiddy Went to Market* (Beder *et al.*, 2009) and wishes that it could be made compulsory reading for all teachers and school leaders. Beder's wide-ranging analysis ranges from 'eatertainment' – the marketing of unsuitable foodstuffs directly at child audiences – to the unapologetic incursion into the production of teaching materials by large profit-driven corporations. The consequence of this, she suggests, is 'the corporate capture of childhood … being felt by children being more materialistic, overweight, stressed, depressed, and self-destructive' (Beder *et al.*, 2009: 223). It is a gloomy vision shared by Sue Palmer in her excellent study *Toxic Childhood* (Palmer, 2006) and Merryn Hutchings's *Exam Factories?* (2015) cited above.

Another prominent campaigner and critic unsettled by the effect of the centrality of testing on our children's welfare is trade union leader Mary Bousted. I meet her on the day she is quoted on the front page of a national newspaper when the government's spending plans on education have been revealed and show an unequivocal commitment to the establishment of more grammar schools. 'We are,' she suggests, 'in a very bad place and I can't imagine it getting any worse.' She points to the fact that a return to timed, linear, end-of-programme examinations is now a fact of life and, like the authors and campaigners cited above, expresses genuine fear about 'endemic, systemic mental health issues' affecting young people. In terms of how this drive may be resisted, she is clear that parental opposition must be incorporated into a wide range of voices. They know, she tells me, that 'it's not about learning, it's about rote-learning and about the grades'. She deplores a 'narrow indigestible curriculum that is too focused on the test'. She points to the possibility that the practicalities of an overloaded examination system – poor quality marking and the difficulty of recruiting suitable assessors, a plethora of administrative errors – may yet lead to a re-think on the part of ministers. She has some optimism that the incumbent at the time of writing, Justine Greening, is a touch more cautious and measured than some of her predecessors.

Bousted sees the debate about testing as one that is intensely political and ideological. She is certain that one of the problems of those campaigning against the current hegemony resides in a lack of confidence in taking on their opponents intellectually, particularly in terms of pedagogic understanding. We begin to talk about the reluctance of politicians to acknowledge any expert view from within the profession (see Chapter 3) but when the name of Nick Gibb crops up, she expresses the view that he is very much an exception. 'He's read his Hirsch, cover to cover,' she suggests. The American critic and commentator E.D. Hirsch Jr. is a figure to be taken seriously by those looking at the curriculum and testing, not least because he currently enjoys cheerleading from a number of educational bloggers and some serious commentators – as well as senior politicians. Hirsch founded the Core Knowledge Foundation (coreknowledge.org) the principal credo of which is that 'only a well-rounded, knowledge-specific curriculum can impart needed knowledge to all children and overcome inequality of opportunity'. He talks of how we are now at a point where we have 'turned schools into soulless test-prep factories, with endless practice of strategies and skills, as they desperately attempt to overcome children's lack of enabling knowledge' (Hirsch, 2016: 8). Bousted talks of how much of what he advocates has a resonance with even left-leaning teachers: the need to address inequality; concepts of knowledge as enabling; real texts rather than excerpts. It can seem attractive but while it is discourteous to contemplate a glib rebuttal, Hirsh's ideas about what constitute the 'core knowledge' stems from ideological principles that can be seen as narrowly geocentric, overly traditional, and casually dismissive of how different people experience life in the 21st century. Bousted's contention, however, is that these ideas need to be confronted in their own terms. The teaching profession and its supporters are 'good at self-righteousness, but less good at taking on the right in their own terms and tackling that'. She talks of how we 'need to know our Vygotsky' and the arguments about setting or the central importance of oracy. In the battle of ideas she believes that we need to be better equipped.

We finish our conversation by turning to our shared belief that teachers remain interested in engaging in such a battle. I point to the results of my research that demonstrates that their spirit has not been quelled and she points to her regular blog in the *Times Educational Supplement* (see tes.com/news/author/mary-bousted) that receives something approaching a quarter of a million 'likes'. The appetite for ideas about education is as keen as ever. We acknowledge that, in her words, for teachers who have 'a 60-hour working week, two-thirds of which have nothing to do with teaching', the generation of such discourse has to be sharp and incisive but that the purpose of engaging in this is to empower teachers to 'push back' against the current system. I express the view that this pushing back probably needs to be expressed in collective action while she appears to favour influencing decision-makers and office holders. We both agree that the potential for creating a national education union will be instrumental in teachers regaining a sense of agency and the emergence of more schools like those featured in this book.

One of the central purposes of this book is to consider the possibilities of resistance to the GERM. In doing so it is necessary to consider the balance of forces. These are teachers, their representative organizations, parent groups and other campaigners on one side; a deeply ideological set of politicians, committed to marketization, commodification and the shrinking of the state on the other. We need to make an objective and sober appraisal of the chances of halting the ideologically driven juggernaut of testing and standardization. This book has looked at schools and settings that are taking brave decisions about putting the child at the centre and trusting to the notion that a broad curriculum and rich, varied exposure to possibilities will, inevitably, lead to success in tests and examinations. At the risk of labouring the point there is no argument here that assessing children is wrong or that dedicating some time to preparing them for examination processes is unacceptable. We have looked at the views of individuals and their organizations who are dedicated to campaigning for change. We have seen how some of these people and the bodies they represent have identified privatization and commercialization as the ideological driving force behind how our schools are run – although this is a view not subscribed to by all of them. The straightforward question remains; what chance of making this oppositional viewpoint the mainstream one? Can we completely change the direction of education discourse that has come from the top for the last 30 years?

The critic Fredric Jameson famously opined that most people can more readily imagine the end of the world than the end of capitalism. The purpose of this book is not to argue that only by overthrowing capitalism can we fight the GERM and put the test in its place – although to be frank it might help. What it does argue for is for all interested parties to use their imagination more vigorously and not to believe that all we have is all there can ever be. If wholesale change is to become the norm, if the GEM is to be eradicated, then three things have to be understood. First, in order to oppose a system that works against the interests of children, we need to understand the ideological drive behind what is happening. In this case it is about those in power cementing a market-driven, privatized and unequal system of educational provision. Second, to borrow from Jameson, it is about having the collective imagination to believe in an alternative system that puts the child – not the data that the child represents – at the centre. Third, it is to understand that political change is a possibility and that ordinary people – teachers, parents, public servants and other workers – can bring about such change. This last point requires further comment.

When finishing *Teachers Undefeated* in the late winter of 2016 I fancifully imagined – although by no means predicted – that by the end of the year Bernie Sanders could be in the White House and Jeremy Corbyn could be challenging to be prime minister. I emphasize that this was nothing more than a vague possibility, and an outside one at that. But it was exactly that – a possibility. It didn't happen and, as it turns out, global events in the following months were even more egregious. The Western world's most powerful nation chose as its leader the star of a reality TV show who exhibited attitudes that many of us thought belonged to a world that had disappeared. In the UK the Brexit vote revealed divisions in society and a mistrust of the political establishment that took many by complete surprise. As I put the finishing touches to this book the global geo-political situation has rarely seemed more fragile and potentially dangerous. The reaction of many people around the world has been to protest, demonstrate and organize. There is a realization that the stakes are high. At the start of the last century activist Rosa Luxemburg famously articulated the idea of society being at the crossroads between socialism or barbarism in times of crisis. Although the campaign against testing may seem small beer in the face of global upheaval, the principle remains the same: only by making opposition collective and widespread can the test be put in its place.

Ultimately, the discussion about the place of testing on the curriculum boils down to a central question: what is education for? For decades this has been a debate about whether education is a liberal humanist project or if its main purpose is the production of human capital. In everyday terms, this asks the question about whether we want a system that produces well-rounded individuals, flexible in their thinking, able to adapt a range of skills to a variety of circumstances – including, but not exclusively about, the world of work – or whether school is about preparing young people to become part of a workforce in a developed economy. There is a paradox here. It is widely accepted that educators and society in general are in a position where we do not know what the jobs of the future look like. As a simple exercise it is worth typing 'preparing young people for jobs that don't exist yet' into a search engine and seeing the array of differing but convincing arguments about this. This is reflected in the views of employers through their mouthpiece, the Confederation of British Industry (CBI). In a report in 2016 the CBI explained that 'by far the most important factor employers weigh up when recruiting school and college leavers is their attitude to work' (CBI, 2016: 6). Eighty-nine per cent of employers rated this as an important quality as opposed to 23 per cent who valued formal qualifications. Other qualities that top the list of requirements are self-management along with the ability to communicate well and analyse situations. In the eight settings explored in this book, along with the discourse that evolves from those interviewed in this final chapter, these are the very qualities that they, too, attempt to foster. It is ironic that even the captains of industry cast doubt on the need to for schools to push for as many pass grades as they can muster. It is perhaps doubly ironic that the CBI choose to have their position published by Pearson, a company whose attempts to corner the global market in educational materials are as stark a warning as any about the unpredictability of marketization and the folly in putting any faith in its reliability (Bond and Khan, 2017).

A book about schools and the purpose of education needs to finish in schools. The idea of the jobs of the future in a future society is a fascinating one. As an English teacher this future was a reliable prompt for imaginative writing. Pupils in the 1970s would speculate with awe about telephones where you could actually *see* the person you were talking to, even if they were on the other side of the world, or of having a TV *on your wrist*. All diseases would be cured by laser beams – whatever they might happen to be. While technological innovations fascinated them, so did one other matter: these advances would be used for our collective benefit so that our only problem would be what to do with the masses of leisure time at our disposal. In a world of precarious, often low-skilled employment, where health care, too, is driven by the market, the question of what education is for could not be more pertinent.

Having finished a conference address with this very point, a retired headteacher approaches me to tell me a story. Her school was in a deprived and difficult part of an inner city and had been bedevilled for some time by local youths stealing cars, swirling them around on the school playground and then setting them on fire. Reluctantly she arranged for some large – and very ugly – concrete blocks to be placed around the playground to act as barriers and for some time this solved the problem. She was dismayed to come in one morning to find a burned out car on the playground and, somehow, the concrete barriers moved. How could this happen? Her investigations revealed that it was the curriculum, her Year 5 teacher, and the Romans who were to blame. It was they, of course, who placed logs under heavy objects to roll them along. It was the Year 5 teacher who taught his class about this and it was they who pinched some stray scaffolding poles to put them under the concrete blocks and roll them away. Test that.

References

Alexander, R. (2004) 'Still no pedagogy? Principle, pragmatism and compliance in primary education'. *Cambridge Journal of Education*, 34 (1), 7–33.

— (2011) 'Legacies, policies and prospects: One year on from the Cambridge Primary Review'. *FORUM*, 53 (1), 71–92.

Althusser, L. (1971) *Lenin and Philosophy, and Other Essays*. Trans. Brewster, B. London: New Left Books.

Apple, M.W. (2004) *Ideology and Curriculum*. 3rd ed. London: Routledge.

Association of Teachers and Lecturers (ATL) (2010) Online. www.atl.org.uk/policy-and-campaigns/conference/2010/conference-2010-gove-speech.asp (accessed 2 June 2016).

Ball, S.J. (1999) *Global Trends in Educational Reform and the Struggle for the Soul of the Teacher!* Paper presented at the British Educational Research Association Annual Conference, University of Sussex, Brighton, 2–5 September. Online. www.leeds.ac.uk/educol/documents/00001212.htm (accessed 30 January 2017).

— (2003) 'The teacher's soul and the terrors of performativity'. *Journal of Education Policy*, 18 (2), 215–28.

— (2008) *The Education Debate*. Bristol: Policy Press.

Barber, M., Moffit, A. and Kihn, P. (2011) *Deliverology 101: A field guide for educational leaders*. Thousand Oaks, CA: Corwin.

Bateman, T. (2017) 'Independent school students gain extra time for exams'. *BBC News*, 10 February. Online. www.bbc.co.uk/news/education-38923034 (accessed 10 February 2017).

BBC (1999) 'Education: Blair blamed over "excuses culture"'. *BBC News*, 21 October. Online. http://news.bbc.co.uk/1/hi/education/480868.stm (accessed 9 February 2017).

Beder, S., Varney, W. and Gosden, R. (2009) *This Little Kiddy Went to Market: The corporate capture of childhood*. London: Pluto Press.

Bennett, M. (2016) 'The schools business'. *London Review of Books* blog, 25 March. Online. www.lrb.co.uk/blog/2016/03/25/matthew-bennett/the-schools-business/ (accessed 3 June 2016).

Berry, J. (2012) 'Does Gove really want to set us free?' *FORUM*, 54 (2), 273–84.

— (2016) *Teachers Undefeated: How global education reform has failed to crush the spirit of educators*. London: Trentham Books.

Berry, J. and Wrigley, T. (2016) *The Mismeasurement of Learning: How tests are damaging children and primary education*. London: National Union of Teachers. Online. https://reclaimingschools.files.wordpress.com/2016/11/mismeasurement.pdf (accessed 13 April 2017).

Black, P. and Wiliam, D. (1998) *Inside the Black Box: Raising standards through classroom assessment*. London: School of Education, King's College London. Online. https://weaeducation.typepad.co.uk/files/blackbox-1.pdf (accessed 13 April 2017).

Boaler, J. (2009) *The Elephant in the Classroom: Helping children learn and love maths*. London: Souvenir Press.

Boaler, J., Wiliam, D. and Brown, M. (2000) 'Students' experiences of ability grouping: Disaffection, polarisation and the construction of failure'. *British Educational Research Journal*, 26 (5), 631–48.

Bond, D. and Khan, M. (2017) 'Pearson shares dive 30% after profit warning'. *Financial Times*, 18 January. Online. www.ft.com/content/008875f8-dd52-11e6-86ac-f253db7791c6 (accessed 2 March 2017).

Boyson, R. (1975) *The Crisis in Education*. London: Woburn Press.

Brannick, T. and Coghlan, D. (2007) 'In defense of being "native": The case for insider academic research'. *Organizational Research Methods*, 10 (1), 59–74.

Braverman, H. (1974) *Labor and Monopoly Capital: The degradation of work in the twentieth century*. London: Monthly Review Press.

Burkard, T. (2008) *Troops to Teachers: A successful programme from America for our inner city schools*. London: Centre for Policy Studies. Online. www.cps.org.uk/files/reports/original/111027170546-20080214PublicServicesTroopsToTeachers.pdf (accessed 13 April 2017).

Carvel, J. (2000) 'Poverty no excuse for failure, says Blunkett'. *The Guardian*, 2 March. Online. www.theguardian.com/uk/2000/mar/02/schools.news1 (accessed 9 February 2017).

Case, P., Case, S. and Catling, S. (2000) 'Please show you're working: A critical assessment of the impact of Ofsted inspection on primary teachers'. *British Journal of Sociology of Education*, 21 (4), 605–21.

CBI (Confederation of British Industry) (2016) *The Right Combination: CBI/ Pearson education and skills survey 2016*. London: Pearson.

Chitty, C. (2011) 'A massive power grab from local communities: The real significance of the 2010 White Paper and the 2011 Education Bill'. *FORUM*, 53 (1), 11–14.

Clare, J. and Jones, G. (2001) 'Blair: Comprehensives have failed'. *The Telegraph*, 13 February. Online. www.telegraph.co.uk/news/uknews/1322418/Blair-comprehensives-have-failed.html (accessed 31 January 2017).

Cox, B. (1995) *Cox on the Battle for the English Curriculum*. London: Hodder and Stoughton.

Cox, C.B. and Boyson, R. (eds) (1975) *Black Paper 1975: The fight for education*. London: J.M. Dent.

Cox, C.B. and Dyson, A.E (eds) (1971) *The Black Papers on Education*. London: Davis-Poynter.

Cunliffe, B. (1975) 'Review: Black Paper 1975'. *New Scientist*, 24 April, 212.

Dale, R. (1989) *The State and Education Policy*. Milton Keynes: Open University Press.

Davies, M. and Edwards, G. (1999) 'Will the curriculum caterpillar ever learn to fly?' *Cambridge Journal of Education*, 29 (2), 265–75.

DCLG (Department for Communities and Local Government) (2015) *The English Indices of Deprivation 2015* (Statistical Release). London: DCLG. Online. www.gov.uk/government/uploads/system/uploads/attachment_data/file/465791/English_Indices_of_Deprivation_2015_-_Statistical_Release.pdf (accessed 7 February 2017).

DfE (Department for Education) (2010) *The Importance of Teaching: The Schools White Paper 2010*. Norwich: The Stationery Office. Online. www.gov.uk/government/uploads/system/uploads/attachment_data/file/175429/CM-7980.pdf (accessed 2 June 2016).

— (2011) *Training Our Next Generation of Outstanding Teachers: An improvement strategy for discussion*. London: DfE. Online. http://media.education.gov.uk/assets/files/pdf/t/training%20our%20next%20generation%20of%20outstanding%20teachers.pdf (accessed 20 February 2017).

— (2014) *Statutory Framework for the Early Years Foundation Stage: Setting the standards for learning, development and care for children from birth to five*. London: DfE. Online. www.gov.uk/government/uploads/system/uploads/attachment_data/file/335504/EYFS_framework_from_1_September_2014__with_clarification_note.pdf (accessed 24 October 2016).

— (2016a) *Behaviour and Discipline in Schools: Advice for headteachers and school staff*. London: DfE. Online. www.gov.uk/government/uploads/system/uploads/attachment_data/file/488034/Behaviour_and_Discipline_in_Schools_-_A_guide_for_headteachers_and_School_Staff.pdf (accessed 3 November 2016).

— (2016b) 'Policy Paper: English Baccalaureate (EBacc)'. Online. www.gov.uk/government/publications/english-baccalaureate-ebacc/english-baccalaureate-ebacc (accessed 26 July 2016).

— (2016c) *School Workforce in England: November 2015*. London: DfE. Online. www.gov.uk/government/statistics/school-workforce-in-england-november-2015 (accessed 10 November 2016).

Foden, M., Fothergill, S. and Gore, T. (2014) *The State of the Coalfields: Economic and social conditions in the former mining communities of England, Scotland and Wales*. Sheffield: Sheffield Hallam University. Online. www4.shu.ac.uk/research/cresr/sites/shu.ac.uk/files/state-of-the-coalfields.pdf (accessed 7 February 2017).

Foster, D. (2017) *Teacher Recruitment and Retention in England* (Briefing Paper 7222). London: House of Commons Library. Online. http://researchbriefings.files.parliament.uk/documents/CBP-7222/CBP-7222.pdf (accessed 6 February 2017).

Freire, P. (1990) *Pedagogy of the Oppressed*. Trans. Bergman Ramos, M. London: Penguin.

Friedman, M. and Friedman, R. (1980) *Free to Choose: A personal statement*. Harmondsworth: Penguin.

Fusch, P.I. and Ness, L.R. (2015) 'Are we there yet? Data saturation in qualitative research'. *The Qualitative Report*, 20 (9), 1408–16.

Gove, M. (2013) 'I refuse to surrender to the Marxist teachers hell-bent on destroying our schools: Education Secretary berates "the new enemies of promise" for opposing his plans'. *Daily Mail*, 23 March. Online. www.dailymail.co.uk/debate/article-2298146/I-refuse-surrender-Marxist-teachers-hell-bent-destroying-schools-Education-Secretary-berates-new-enemies-promise-opposing-plans.html#ixzz4ZQOblM5g (accessed 22 February 2017).

The Guardian (n.d.) Warwick Mansell profile. Online. www.theguardian.com/profile/warwick-mansell (accessed 28th February 2017).

Harris, S. (2014) 'Bonfire of "soft" GCSEs: Media studies, astronomy and tourism could be axed in bid to make qualification more rigorous'. *Daily Mail*, 1 June. www.dailymail.co.uk/news/article-2645486/Michael-Gove-set-axe-soft-GCSEs-including-media-studies-astronomy-tourism-bid-make-qualification-rigorous.html (accessed 26 July 2016).

Harvey, D. (2005) *A Brief History of Neoliberalism*. Oxford: Oxford University Press.

Hirsch, E.D. (2016) *Why Knowledge Matters: Rescuing our children from failed educational theories*. Cambridge, MA: Harvard Education Press.

Holt, M. (2014) 'Slow education: Possibilities for research and development'. *Local Schools Network*, 1 April. Online. www.localschoolsnetwork.org.uk/2014/04/slow-education-possibilities-for-research-and-development (accessed 28 February 2017).

Hutchings, M. (2015) *Exam Factories? The impact of accountability measures on children and young people*. London: National Union of Teachers. Online. www.teachers.org.uk/files/exam-factories.pdf (accessed 13 April 2017).

Illich, I. (1976) *Deschooling Society*. Harmondsworth: Penguin.

ISC (Independent Schools Council) (2016) 'Exam results 2016'. Online. www.isc.co.uk/research/exam-results/exam-results-2016/ (accessed 27th October 2016).

ISC (Independent Schools Council) (2017) Research section. Online. www.isc.co.uk/research/ (accessed 20th April 2017).

Jarvis, P. (2016) 'Too much, too young for PISA'. *Huffington Post*, 9 December. Online. www.huffingtonpost.co.uk/pam-jarvis/too-much-too-young-for-pi_b_13479730.html (accessed 21 December 2016).

Jeffreys, B. (2015) 'Rising number of pupils home educated'. *BBC News*, 21 December. Online. www.bbc.co.uk/news/education-35133119 (accessed 13 October 2016).

Johnson, R. (1991) 'A new road to serfdom? A critical history of the 1988 Act'. In Education Group II, University of Birmingham (eds) *Education Limited: Schooling, training and the New Right in England since 1979*. London: Unwin Hyman, 31–86.

Kennedy, M. (2014) 'To Kill a Mockingbird and Of Mice and Men axed as Gove orders more Brit lit'. *The Guardian*, 25 May. Online. www.theguardian.com/education/2014/may/25/mockingbird-mice-and-men-axed-michael-gove-gcse (accessed 31 January 2017).

Kraftl, P. (2013) 'Towards geographies of "alternative" education: A case study of UK home schooling families'. *Transactions of the Institute of British Geographers*, 38 (3), 436–50.

Lees, H.E. (2014) *Education without Schools: Discovering alternatives*. Bristol: Policy Press.

Lightfoot, L. (2016) 'Nearly half of England's teachers plan to leave in next five years'. *The Guardian*, 22 March. Online. www.theguardian.com/education/2016/mar/22/teachers-plan-leave-five-years-survey-workload-england (accessed 25 July 2016).

Major, L.E. (2014) 'Teaching matters more than setting'. Sutton Trust blog, 11 December. Online. www.suttontrust.com/newsarchive/teaching-matters-more-than-setting/ (accessed 25 January 2017).

References

Mansell, W. (2007) *Education by Numbers: The tyranny of testing*. London: Politico's.

OECD (Organisation for Economic Co-operation and Development) (2016) *PISA 2015 Results in Focus*. Paris: OECD. Online. www.oecd.org/pisa/pisa-2015-results-in-focus.pdf (accessed 21 March 2017).

Ofsted (2012) *Moving English Forward: Action to raise standards in English*. Manchester: Ofsted. Online. www.gov.uk/government/uploads/system/uploads/attachment_data/file/181204/110118.pdf (accessed 21 December 2016).

Osborne, G. (2016) 'Budget 2016: George Osborne's speech'. Online. www.gov.uk/government/speeches/budget-2016-george-osbornes-speech (accessed 3 June 2016).

Palmer, S. (2006) *Toxic Childhood: How the modern world is damaging our children and what we can do about it*. London: Orion.

Patton, M.Q. (1990) *Qualitative Evaluation and Research Methods*. 2nd ed. Newbury Park, CA: SAGE Publications.

Perryman, J. (2006) 'Panoptic performativity and school inspection regimes: Disciplinary mechanisms and life under special measures'. *Journal of Education Policy*, 21 (2), 147–61.

Postman, N. and Weingartner, C. (1969) *Teaching as a Subversive Activity*. New York: Dell Publishing.

Richardson, H. (2016) 'Troops to Teachers sees 28 ex-servicemen qualify'. *BBC News*, 18 February. Online. www.bbc.co.uk/news/education-35595424 (accessed 4 November 2016).

Sahlberg, P. (2012) *Finnish Lessons: What can the world learn from educational change in Finland?* New York: Teachers College Press.

Sammons, P. and Bakkum, L. (2011) 'Effective schools, equity and teacher effectiveness: A review to the literature'. *Profesorado*, 15 (3), 9–26.

Shulruf, B. (2010) 'Do extra-curricular activities in schools improve educational outcomes? A critical review and meta-analysis of the literature'. *International Review of Education*, 56 (5–6), 591–612.

Simon, B. (1994) 'Why no pedagogy in England?' In Moon, B. and Shelton Mayes, A. (eds) *Teaching and Learning in the Secondary School*. London: Routledge, 10–22.

Storey, A. (2009) 'How fares the "new professionalism" in schools? Findings from the "State of the Nation" project'. *Curriculum Journal*, 20 (2), 121–38.

Sukhnandan, L. and Lee, B. (1998) *Streaming, Setting and Grouping by Ability: A review of the literature*. Slough: National Foundation for Educational Research. Online. www.nfer.ac.uk/publications/SSG01/SSG01.pdf (accessed 25 January 2017).

Sutton Trust (2016) 'Education backgrounds of Olympic medallists'. Online. www.suttontrust.com/researcharchive/education-backgrounds-of-olympic-medallists/ (accessed 27 October 2016).

Swann, M., Peacock, A., Hart, S. and Drummond, M.J. (2012) *Creating Learning without Limits*. Maidenhead: Open University Press.

Szamuely, T. (1971) 'Russia and Britain: Comprehensive inequality'. In Cox, C.B. and Dyson, A.E (eds) *The Black Papers on Education*. London: Davis-Poynter, 121–38.

UK Government (2016) *Education and Adoption Act 2016*. London: The Stationery Office. Online. www.legislation.gov.uk/ukpga/2016/6/contents/enacted (accessed 3 June 2016).

UK Parliament (2016) 'Primary assessment inquiry launched'. *Education Committee News*, 23 September. Online. www.parliament.uk/business/committees/committees-a-z/commons-select/education-committee/news-parliament-2015/primary-assessment-launch-16-17/ (accessed 13 April 2017).

University of Warwick (2015) *Enriching Britain: Culture, creativity and growth* (Warwick Commission on the Future of Cultural Value 2015 Report). Coventry: University of Warwick. Online. www2.warwick.ac.uk/research/warwickcommission/futureculture/finalreport/warwick_commission_final_report.pdf (accessed 28 October 2016).

Walker, M., Bartlett, S., Betts, H., Sainsbury, M. and Worth, J. (2014) *Phonics Screening Check Evaluation*. London: DfE.

Watt, N. and Wintour, P. (2014) 'David Cameron axes Michael Gove in reshuffle after toxic poll warning'. *The Guardian*, 15 July. Online. www.theguardian.com/politics/2014/jul/15/cameron-sacks-toxic-gove-promotes-women-reshuffle (accessed 2 June 2016).

Weale, S. (2016) 'Thousands of children miss out on first-choice secondary school'. *The Guardian*, 1 March. Online. www.theguardian.com/education/2016/mar/01/thousands-of-children-miss-out-on-first-choice-secondary-school (accessed 2 June 2016).

Williams, R. (1961) *The Long Revolution*. Harmondsworth: Penguin.

Williamson, B. (2014) 'Reassembling children as data doppelgängers: How databases are making education machine-readable'. Paper prepared for the Powerful Knowledge Conference, University of Bristol, 16 May. Online. http://tinyurl.com/z8tzjwv (accessed 22 February 2017).

YouTube (2017) 'Gove: Britons have had enough of experts'. Online. www.youtube.com/watch?v=GGgiGtJk7MA (accessed 20 February 2017).

Index